DRONE WARFARE

KILLING BY REMOTE CONTROL

Medea Benjamin

HarperCollins *Publishers* India

First published in the US by OR Books, New York and London 2012

This edition published in India
by HarperCollins *Publishers* in 2013

HarperCollins Publishers India, Cyber City, Building 10-A, Gurugram,
Haryana-122002, India
www.harpercollins.co.in

2 4 6 8 10 9 7 5 3

P-ISBN: 978-93-5029-991-3
E-ISBN: 978-93-5029-992-0

Typeset in 12/16 Utopia Std
by Ram Das Lal, New Delhi

Printed and bound at
MicroPrints India, New Delhi

MIX
Paper
FSC FSC® C218906

This product is made of FSC®-certified and other controlled material.

HarperCollins Publishers, Macken House, 39/40 Mayor Street
Upper, Dublin 1, D01 C9W8, Ireland

DRONE WARFARE

Tighe Barry

Medea Benjamin is a co-founder of the peace group CODEPINK and the international human rights organization Global Exchange. She has been an advocate for social justice for more than thirty years. Described as 'one of America's most committed—and most effective—fighters for human rights' by New York *Newsday*, and called 'one of the high profile leaders of the peace movement' by *The Los Angeles Times*, Benjamin is the author/editor of eight books. A former economist and nutritionist with the United Nations and World Health Organization, Benjamin's articles appear regularly in publications such as *The Huffington Post*, *Common Dreams*, *Alternet* and *OpEd News*.

Table of Contents

Foreword

In many ways, drones present the same moral issues as any other action-at-a-distance weapon: They allow warriors to kill at a minimal risk to themselves, thus lowering the human cost of aggression. Thus the ancient contempt for archers, as recounted in *The Iliad,* where the Greek chieftains deride the Trojan prince Paris for his reliance on the bow and arrow. Real men are not afraid of hand-to-hand combat; only cowards attack from a distance, often hiding behind trees or rocks.

Drones are of course the ultimate action-at-a-distance weapons, allowing the aggressor to destroy targets in Pakistan or Afghanistan while 'hiding' thousands of miles away in Nevada. But this alone does not make them uniquely pernicious: Missiles and aerial bombardment can also be launched from great distances by individuals who need not see the extent of the violence they inflict. If we are to end war, we need to take aim at all the weaponry that makes it possible and even inviting—guns, artillery, fighter planes and bombs—and at the industries that manufacture them.

But in this remarkably cogent and carefully researched book, Medea Benjamin makes it clear that drones are not just another example of high-tech military trinket. In fact, it is hard to even claim that their primary use is 'military' in any traditional sense. Drones have made possible a program of targeted assassinations that are justified by the US 'war on terror,' but otherwise in defiance of both international and US law. As Benjamin documents, it is the CIA, not the Pentagon, that operates most drone strikes in Western Asia, with no accountability whatsoever. Designated targets, including American citizens, have been condemned without evidence or trial—at the will, apparently, of the White House. And those who operate the drones do so with complete impunity for the deaths of any civilians who end up as collateral damage.

One of Benjamin's most disturbing revelations has to do with the explosive expansion of the drone industry in just the last few years, to the point where fifty nations now possess the devices. *Drone Warfare* sketches out the nightmare possibilities posed by this insane proliferation. Not only can we can expect drones to fall into the hands of 'rogue' nations or terrorist groups; we should brace ourselves, too, for the domestic use of surveillance drones and even armed drones at the Mexican border and possibly against American civilian protestors.

In anyone else's hands, this could be a deeply depressing book. Fortunately though, Medea Benjamin is not just an ace reporter; she's one of the world's leading anti-war activists. *Drone Warfare* ends with the story of the global anti-drone movement, in which she has played a central role. At the end of this book, you'll be inspired—and you'll know exactly how to get involved!

— Barbara Ehrenreich
Alexandria,VA, January 2012

Introduction

I met Roya on my first day while visiting the Pakistan-Afghan border, on a dusty road in Peshawar. It was just weeks after the 2002 US invasion of Afghanistan, and I was traveling as a representative of the human rights group I co-founded called Global Exchange. A young girl approached me, her head cocked to one side, her hand outstretched, begging for money.

With the help of an interpreter, I learned her story. Roya was thirteen years old, the same age as my youngest daughter. But her life could not have been in starker contrast to that of my San Francisco high schooler and her girlfriends. Roya never had time for sports, or for school. Born into a poor family living on the outskirts of Kabul, her father was a street vendor. Her mother raised five children and baked sweets for him to sell.

One day while her father was out selling candies, Roya and her two sisters were trudging home carrying buckets of water. Suddenly, they heard a terrifying whir and then there was an explosion: something terrible had dropped from the sky, tearing their house apart and sending the body parts of their mother and two brothers flying through the air.

The Americans must have thought Roya's home was part of a nearby Taliban housing compound. In the cold vernacular of military-speak, her family had become 'collateral damage' in America's war on terror.

When Roya's father came home, he carefully collected all the bits and pieces of his pulverized family that he could find, buried them immediately according to Islamic tradition, and then sank into a severe state of shock.

Roya became the head of her household. She bundled up her surviving sisters, grabbed her father, and fled. With no money or provisions, they trekked through the Hindu Kush, across the Khyber Pass, and into Pakistan.

Once in Peshawar, the family barely survived on the one dollar a day the girls made from begging. Roya took me to their one-room adobe hut to meet her father. A tall, strong man with the calloused hands of a hard worker, he no longer works. He doesn't even walk or talk. He just sits and stares into space. 'Once in a while he smiles,' Roya whispered.

Inside Afghanistan, I saw more lives destroyed by US bombs. Some bombs hit the right target but caused horrific collateral damage. Some bombs hit the wrong target because of human error, machine malfunction or faulty information. In one village, the Americans thought a wedding party was a Taliban gathering. One minute, forty-three relatives were joyously celebrating; the next minute, their appendages were hanging off the limbs of trees.

Forty villagers were killed in another small town in the middle of the night. Their crime? They lived near the caves of Tora Bora, where Osama bin Laden was presumed to be hiding. The US news media reported the dead as Taliban militants. But the woman I met—who had just lost her husband and four children, as well as both her legs—had never heard of Al Qaeda, America or George Bush. Bleeding profusely, she was praying that she would die. Surviving as a crippled widow with no income and no family was too much to bear.

Unknown to most Americans, in just three months between October 7, 2001 and January 1, 2002, over 1,000 Afghan civilians were directly killed by the US-led bombing campaign and at least 3,200 more had died of 'starvation, exposure, associated illnesses, or injury sustained while in flight from war zones,' according to the Project on Defense Alternatives.[1] This is more than the number of people killed in the 9/11 attacks.

President Bush had choices after the dreadful events of 9/11/2001. He could have treated the attacks as a crime against humanity that required internationally coordinated police work to capture the perpetrators and bring them to justice. Instead, he chose ground invasions by heavily armed troops and aerial attacks that sent thousands of bombs and missiles screeching through the skies.

The American government told the public not to worry about who was on the receiving end of the air attacks.

We were getting rid of the Taliban, which was indeed a vicious government. And the US military now had smart bombs and laser-guided missiles that, together with a newfangled kind of unmanned planes called drones, gave them the capability of dropping munitions with breath-taking precision. Government officials insisted that Al Qaeda militants who attacked the United States or who were plotting future attacks—together with their Taliban supporters—would get what they deserved, while civilian casualties would be carefully avoided.

When I realized this was a lie, I vowed that I would try to get the US government to help compensate these innocent victims of our attacks. I also vowed that I would never allow myself to be lulled into thinking that high-tech wars were somehow more humane.

Then came the March 2003 invasion of Iraq, a war based on lies about Saddam Hussein's purported involvement in 9/11 and the 'imminent threat' he posed to the United States because of his supposed possession of weapons of mass destruction. The US military bragged that unlike the 1991 Gulf War, where 93 percent of the munitions dropped were 'dumb' bombs, 70 percent of the munitions dropped a dozen years later were laser-guided 'smart' bombs or precision missiles.[2] Expect minimal collateral damage, we were told.

I must admit that when I walked down the streets of Baghdad a few months after the invasion, I marveled at the selective destruction of those weapons. Block after block, I saw one building reduced to rubble while the building right next to it was standing tall. With high-tech munitions, the military was able to zoom in on key targets: government ministries, the country's electrical grid, water treatment plants, sewage systems, food storage facilities, bus depots, bridges, communication centers. But precise targeting, Iraqis told us, did not necessarily minimize casualties. What about the workers in those buildings? What about the people who happened to be walking by? And what about the hundreds of thousands of Iraqis, mostly children, who died from the subsequent lack of clean water and healthcare? All this callous destruction occurred in a country that had nothing to do with Al Qaeda or 9/11.

Back in the US, I worked with Global Exchange to create a Congressional fund for compensating innocent victims of our attacks. Our staffperson Marla Ruzicka, one of the most compassionate and passionate young women I have ever met, worked feverishly on this, later founding a group called CIVIC, Campaign for Innocent Victims in Conflict. Tragically, in April 2005, Marla was killed by a roadside bomb in Iraq; she was just 28. A compensation fund created by Congress in her name has distributed over $40 million to the families and communities of innocent victims.

While it was important to help the people we mistakenly harm, I felt it was more important to stop the wars. Together with my colleague Jodie Evans, we founded the women-led peace group CODEPINK. We believed that individuals who attacked our nation on 9/11 had to be captured and brought to justice, but that 9/11 did not justify going to war. Yes, the Taliban were oppressive, especially to women, but Western military intervention was not the right path to liberation.

We also urged our government to examine how our military presence around the world, with over eight hundred overseas bases, was fueling anti-American sentiment (it was one of the reasons Osama bin Laden gave for the 9/11 attacks). We insisted that the United States could save much-needed money, and make our nation safer, by closing those bases and using the military for protection at home.

We organized huge rallies, engaged in civil disobedience, traveled to war zones to get first-hand experience, and went on grueling hunger strikes calling for the withdrawal of our troops from Iraq and Afghanistan and for investing the creative energy of the international community into peacemaking, with women from the affected countries having a prominent seat at the table. We also called for an overhaul of another misguided US policy, the one-sided support for the government of Israel—a position that violates the human rights of Palestinians and inflames the very anti-Americanism that fuels terrorist attacks.

Despite our efforts, it became clear that the Bush administration would not budge. So during the 2008 presidential campaign, many anti-war activists threw themselves into the election of Barack Obama, only to discover that the peace candidate had morphed into the war president. While President Obama withdrew our troops from Iraq in December 2011 (he was actually forced to do so by an agreement signed under President Bush), he escalated the number of troops in Afghanistan.

He also chose another tactic that would help keep the war far removed from public consciousness: drone warfare. An aircraft that kills by remote control—also known by sophisticated names like unmanned aerial vehicle (UAV), unmanned aircraft system (UAS) and remotely piloted aircraft (RPA)—became the weapon of choice.

Members of the US peace community watched in horror as these snipers in the sky started spreading from Afghanistan and Iraq to Pakistan, Yemen, Somalia, the Philippines and Libya. Instead of stopping the scourge of war, under Nobel Peace Prize winner President Obama the military was simply shifting tactics from boots on the ground to assassins in the air.

In fact, President Obama carried out his first drone strike just three days after his inauguration. It was in Pakistan on January 23, 2009. Initial reports said that the attacks struck 'suspected terrorist hideouts,' but in reality the missiles struck the home of Malik Gulistan Khan, a tribal elder and member of a local pro-government peace committee, and killed him and four other family members. 'I lost my father, three brothers, and my cousin in this attack,' said Adnan, his eighteen-year-old son. Adnan's uncle claimed, 'We did nothing, have no connection to militants at all. Our family supported the government and in fact...was a member of a local peace committee.' Reports later confirmed the family's story.[3]

You would think this tragedy would have been enough to make President Obama reconsider the policy. It wasn't. In fact, it was only years later, during a 'Google chat' on January 30, 2012, that Obama even admitted to the public that the US had a covert drone program in Pakistan. Responding to a comment about drone strikes killing innocent people, Obama tried to reassure the public that they need not worry about dead civilians. 'Drones have not caused a huge number of civilian casualties. For the most part, they have been precision strikes on Al Qaeda and their affiliates,' he told his listeners. 'It is important to understand that this thing is being kept on a very tight leash.'

But a jaw-dropping May 2012 *New York Times* report showed a president who had weekly meetings with his advisors on 'Terror Tuesdays' to look at profiles of terror suspects much as one would flip through baseball cards, and 'nominate' people to be on a kill list.[4] The president was reportedly able to approve lethal action 'without hand-wringing'—even the decision to put an American cleric in Yemen on the kill list was 'an easy one.' Most shocking of all, the report made clear why the administration was able to claim such a low civilian death count: It automatically defines as a combatant any male of military age who lives in the area where the US is using drones, 'unless there is explicit intelligence posthumously proving them innocent.' So a principle of innocent until proven guilty has morphed into a policy of guilty, and dead, until proven innocent. (And even this possibility of a posthumous declaration of innocence is a cruel joke, since the US makes little effort to identify all those killed or injured, much less investigate their backgrounds.)

Instead of a massive outcry from the American public, polls found overwhelming support. A February

2012 *Washington Post*/ABC opinion poll asking people if they approved of the use of drones against 'terrorist suspects overseas' showed an approval rate of 83 percent. This included not only a majority of Republicans and independents, but Democrats and people who self-defined as liberal Democrats. A clear majority of 79 percent even approved of using drones against American citizens overseas.[5]

Three months later, a June 2012 Pew Research Center poll found less support for drone strikes—62 percent—but still comprising a majority of Americans. However, Pew also polled twenty other countries and found just the reverse: from Germany to Mexico to China, the world said no to US drones. In US-friendly Muslim nations such as Egypt, Jordan and Turkey the disapproval rates were enormous, ranging from 81 to 89 percent.[6]

Unlike US officials and a bamboozled US public, most people around the world do not believe that the United States—or any nation—has the right to attack whomever it wants, wherever it wants. People on the receiving end of drone missiles began rising up in protest. So did members of the peace community in the United States—including groups like my organization CODEPINK, Voices for Creative Nonviolence, and Catholic Workers—as well as activists in Europe and Australia. They were joined by scientists, ethicists, and other professionals alarmed by the explosion in the use of robotic warfare, particularly lethal drones.

Together, they are part of a growing chorus demanding an international dialogue about the direction, ethics, and legality of high-tech warfare. More and more, people of conscience are calling for international guidelines to curb robotic warfare, as the world community has done in the case of land mines and cluster bombs.

This book, dedicated to Roya and all the innocent victims of drone warfare, is meant to move that process along.

1

A Sordid Love Affair with Killer Drones

At the 2004 Radio and Television Correspondents' Dinner, President Bush joked about searching for weapons of mass destruction under Oval Office furniture, since they had never been found in Iraq. The joke backfired when parents who had lost their children fighting in Iraq said they found it offensive and tasteless. Senator John Kerry said Bush displayed a 'stunningly cavalier' attitude toward the war and those fighting it.

Six years later, at the White House Correspondents' Dinner, President Obama made his own not-so-funny joke about weapons and war. When the pop band Jonas Brothers was about to play to the packed room, Obama furrowed his brow and sent them a warning to keep away from his daughters. 'Sasha and Malia are huge fans, but boys, don't get any ideas. Two words for you: Predator drones. You'll never see it coming.'

For people in Pakistan, where American drones have been dropping their Hellfire missiles, Obama's joke lost something in translation. According to Pakistani journalist Khawar Rizvi, few Pakistanis had ever heard of the Jonas Brothers or understood the reference to the president's daughters. 'But one thing we do know: There's nothing funny about Predator drones,' said Rizvi.[7]

That seemed to be the opinion of Faisal Shahzad, a thirty-year-old Pakistan-born resident of Bridgeport, Connecticut. On May 1, 2010, just one day after President Obama made his offensive drone joke, Shahzad tried to set off a car bomb in New York City's Times Square. The would-be bomber had left his explosive-laden Nissan Pathfinder parked in the middle of the busiest intersection in New York City at the busiest time: 6:30 p.m. on a Saturday night. Luckily, the bomb failed to explode, and the authorities—tipped off by local t-shirt vendors—disarmed it before it caused any casualties.

Questioned about his motives by the authorities, Shahzad talked about US drone attacks killing children in Pakistan and Afghanistan.

'You know what would have made a great punch line for Barack Obama's joke about Predator drones last night at the White House correspondents' dinner?' suggested writer Jonathan Schwarz after hearing about the bomb scare.[8] 'If the car bomb in Times Square had gone off at exactly that moment, and it turned out it was, in fact, in retaliation for strikes by Predator drones. Then the next night, when they were still washing blood and viscera off the streets of New York, the head of the Pakistani Taliban could have made a quip about killing people with car bombs at a fancy black tie dinner in Peshawar. And then the US could have blown up more Pakistani civilians with drones. And the cycle of funniness would begin anew!'

Some say the name 'drone' comes from the constant buzzing noise that some of the machines make in flight. According to other military lore, the name derives from a use of robotic aircraft as training targets for World War II gun crews.[9] The United States manufactured 15,000 small drones for anti-aircraft practice during the war at a plant in southern California. Many were marked with black stripes along the tail part of the fuselage, making them look like drones (the bees).

The technology for flying remotely has existed for decades. Unmanned aerial vehicles were first tested by the military way back during World War I. In the 1930s, the US, the UK, and Germany, later joined by the USSR and others, all began to use drones for anti-aircraft targeting exercises. Unmanned crafts were used as guided missiles by the US military in World War II and the Korean War. In a tragic World War II experiment gone awry, President Kennedy's older brother Joe, a Navy pilot, died at age 29 in a secret drone operation against the Germans. It wasn't until the Vietnam War that unmanned aircraft were used to gather intelligence.[10]

Anyone who wants to build an unmanned aircraft can order the parts online and assemble them in their garage.

By October 2012, the US-based do-it-yourself drones group, DIY Drones, had over 30,000 members.

The prototype for the most popular killer drone, the Predator, was built by Israeli aviation engineer Abraham Karem in his garage in southern California in the 1980s.[11]

Abraham Karem had worked on developing unmanned aircraft for an Israeli defense contractor in the 1970s, and then moved to southern California in 1980 to develop his own company.

With grants from the US military's Defense Advanced Research Projects Agency (DARPA) and the CIA, Karem began building a new model at home in his three-car garage. In 1981 he unveiled what he called the Albatross, an unmanned plane that could stay in the air for up to 56 hours, and later a new version with a powerful flight control computer called the Gnat 750.

But Karem was financially strapped and decided to sell his company to Hughes Aircraft, which then sold it to General Atomics, keeping Karem on as a consultant.

In 1993 CIA director James Woolsey, unhappy with the intelligence he was receiving from satellites flying over Bosnia, turned to Karem and General Atomics for help. A year later, the Gnat 750 was flying over Bosnia with a crew that was not in the aircraft but launching it from an abandoned airfield in neighboring Albania.

The data it gathered still had a circuitous path to reach the CIA—traveling from the drone to a manned aircraft to a ground station to a satellite. So the engineers re-rigged the drone with its own satellite communications system, adding the now characteristic bulbous nose to the fuselage.

Thus the Predator drone was born and was used in the Balkan wars to gather information on refugee flows and Serbian air defenses. It was not until the 1999 NATO Kosovo campaign, however, that someone came up with the idea of equipping these planes with missiles, transforming them from spy planes into killer drones.[12]

Today drones are used for both lethal and non-lethal purposes. Outside the military, unmanned aircraft are being drafted for everything from tracking drug smugglers and monitoring the US–Mexico border to engaging in search operations after earthquakes and spraying pesticides on crops. Environmentalists are using them to catch illegal whalers and illegal loggers. The potential commercial uses are endless, from delivering packages to delivering tacos. And you can buy your own miniature drone on Amazon.com for $300 and control with it your smartphone. But the driving force behind the most sophisticated drones, and the source of immense funds for research and devlopment, is the military.

The Israeli military has a long history of using drones to gather intelligence, as decoys, and for targeted killings. Their use of drones dates back to the occupation of the Sinai in the 1970s, and was further developed in the 1982 war in Lebanon and the ongoing conflicts in the Palestinian territories.

The Israeli unmanned aircraft pioneered in the late 1970s and 1980s were eventually integrated into the United States' inventory. Impressed with Israel's use of UAVs during military operations in Lebanon in 1982, then Navy Secretary John Lehman decided to acquire

UAV capability for the Navy. One of the UAVs purchased from Israel, the Pioneer, was used to gather intelligence during Desert Storm. According to a Congressional Research Report in 2003, 'Following the Gulf War, military officials recognized the worth of UAVs, and the Air Force's Predator became a UAV on a fast track, quickly adding new capabilities.'[13]

But it was the 9/11 World Trade Center attacks that led to an explosion in the US military's use of drones and a host of other robotic weapons. The hundreds of billions of dollars that Congress allocated for the wars in Afghanistan and Iraq made the Pentagon flush with funds to buy up all manner of robotic weapons that military contractors from General Atomics to Northrop Grumman had been developing.

The various branches of the military filled their shopping carts with every robot they could find: tiny surveillance robots that can climb walls and stairs, snake-like robots that slither in the grass, unmanned tanks mounted with .50 caliber weapons, and ground robots to carry the soldiers' heavy loads.

They snatched up every type of drone on the production lines and commissioned new ones. They bought the 38-inch-long Raven that is launched by simply throwing it into the air; the 27-foot-long Predator with its Hellfire missiles, and later the more powerful Reaper version; the 40-foot-long Global Hawk with sci-fi surveillance capabilities.

The Pentagon was ordering these machines faster than the companies could produce them. In 2000, the

Pentagon had fewer than fifty aerial drones; ten years later, it had nearly 7,500. Most of these were mini-drones for battlefield surveillance, but they also had about 800 of the bigger drones, ranging in size from a private aircraft to a commercial jet. Then Secretary of Defense Robert Gates said that the next generation of fighter jet, the F-35 that took decades to develop at a cost of more than $500 million each, would be the Pentagon's last manned fighter aircraft.[14]

From 2002–2010, the Department of Defense's unmanned aircraft inventory increased more than forty-fold.[15] Even during the financial crisis that started brewing in 2007 and led to the slashing of government programs from nutrition supplements for pregnant women to maintenance of national parks, the Defense Department kept pouring buckets of money into drones. At the height of government deficit-reducing cuts in 2012, the US taxpayer was shelling out $3.9 billion for the procurement of unmanned aircraft, not counting the separate drone budgets for the CIA and the Department of Homeland Security.[16]

Most military drones are still used for surveillance purposes. The photo sensors the UAVs carry have become increasingly powerful, allowing the on-the-ground pilots to watch individuals from an aircraft 30,000–60,000 feet up in the air. The infrared and ultraviolet imaging captures light outside the spectrum visible to the human eye. UV imaging is useful in space and for tracking rockets; IR imaging shows heat emitted by an object, making it ideal for identifying humans in the dark.

One reason for the great demand in drones was that they

graduated from simply tracking and monitoring targets to actually killing them. In Afghanistan, drones were credited for killing senior Al Qaeda and Taliban militants. In the Iraq invasion, they were used for everything from tracking supporters of Saddam Hussein to blowing up government agencies. In 2003, US Air Force Chief of Staff General T. Michael Moseley said, 'We've moved from using UAVs primarily in intelligence, surveillance, and reconnaissance roles before Operation Iraqi Freedom, to a true hunter-killer role.'[17]

Another reason that drones were in such demand was the very nature of the Afghan and Iraqi wars. The US military had a hard time even finding its enemies, as many local fighters blended in among the civilian populations. Drones gave the military a way to conduct persistent surveillance and to strike quickly.

Armed drones are used in three ways. They supply air support when US ground troops attack or come under attack; they patrol the skies looking for suspicious activity and, if they find it, they attack; and they conduct targeted killings of suspected militants.

The main advantage of using drones is precisely that they are unmanned. With the operators safely tucked in air-conditioned rooms far away, there's no pilot at risk of being killed or maimed in a crash. No pilot to be taken captive by enemy forces. No pilot to cause a diplomatic crisis if shot down in a 'friendly country' while bombing or spying without official permission. If a drone crashes or is shot down, the pilot back home can simply get up and take a coffee break.

Drones are considered ideal for '3D missions'—actions that are too 'dull, dirty, or dangerous' for manned aircraft. On daring missions, they can fly low and slow over hostile terrain, hovering for several hours or all day, if need be. With their astonishing sensors, from several miles in the air they can follow the route of a suspicious-looking pick-up truck or track a sniper on a rooftop. The Predator's infrared camera can even identify the heat signature of a human body from 10,000 feet in the air. From 8,000 miles away in Nevada, a drone pilot can watch an Afghan as he lights up cigarettes, sits talking to friends on a park bench, or goes to the bathroom—never imagining that anyone is watching him.

Without the need to provide space for aircrew, and without a human crew to become tired, unmanned aircraft can have extremely long endurance. The Reaper can linger in the air for about eighteen hours and hybrid air vehicles have an endurance of weeks. In July 2012, Lockheed Martin announced that it had successfully completed an indoor flight test using laser power to recharge its electric drone, the Stalker, in midair. In the future, high-altitude UAVs using solar power—or powered by ground-based lasers, or using air-to-air refueling—will be able to remain airborne indefinitely.

Unmanned aircraft can fly to remote areas where our troops, and those of the host country, are unable or unwilling to go. They can share data immediately with troops on the ground. They can weave and dive and perform high-speed aerobatics that would cause a human pilot to lose consciousness.

Drone proponents insist that their ability to linger for hours over their target allows for a thorough assessment of potential collateral damage before acting, and their ability to guide weapons to designated targets with pinpoint accuracy means fewer civilian casualties. Certainly, compared to the carpet bombing of World War II or the aerial bombardment of Vietnam or even the 'dumb bombs' used by the US military in the Gulf War, drone missiles are more precise—but these same missiles can be used by manned aircraft.

Drones are also significantly cheaper to purchase than the manned aircraft they are replacing. Lockheed Martin's F-22 fighter jets cost around $150 million apiece, while F-35s clock in at $90 million and the F-16s at $55 million. By contrast, the 2011 price of the Predator was $5 million and the Reaper was $28.4 million—but the (slow, vulnerable) Reaper hardly replaces the (fast, stealthy, air-air combat dominant) F-22.[18]

Even these figures can be misleading. The cost of fueling, operating and maintaining drones is not fully known, as the CIA, which is responsible for their increasing use in undeclared wars in places like Pakistan and Yemen, includes those costs in its classified 'black budget.' But every hour a drone is up in the air is estimated to cost between $2,000 and $3,500, and the number of flight hours has skyrocketed. Between 2001–2010 the time the Air Force devoted to flying missions went up 3,000 percent. The Defense Department reported clocking in 10,000 UAV flight hours in 2005; by 2010 that number was more than 550,000. In Afghanistan and Iraq, Predators and Reapers were in the air 24/7. And they were firing thousands of Hellfire missiles at $68,000 a pop.

A huge cost associated with drones is personnel. While it might seem counterintuitive, it takes significantly more people to operate unmanned aircraft than it does to fly traditional warplanes. According to the Air Force, it takes a jaw-dropping 168 people to keep just one Predator aloft for twenty-four hours! For the larger Global Hawk surveillance drone, that number jumps to 300 people. In contrast, an F-16 fighter aircraft needs fewer than one hundred people per mission.[19]

UAVs need constant attention and control from ground crew. They need ground-based pilots and crews for take-off and landing, ground-based technicians and mechanics to maintain the heavily used aircraft, crews back in the US for piloting and operating the sensors. On top of that, they need intelligence analysts to scrutinize nonstop surveillance feeds and to analyze the massive amount of data they generate. Every day, the Air Force alone processes almost 1,500 hours of full-motion video and another 1,500 still images. By 2010, this required about nineteen analysts per drone.[20]

This information overload will get significantly more labor intensive with use of even more sophisticated technology, such as the 'Gorgon Stare' that can video an entire city, requiring 2,000 analysts to process the data feeds from but a single drone.[21] By 2011, the Air Force had already converted seven Air National Guard squadrons into intelligence units to help analyze drone video and was training an additional 2,000 Air Force intelligence analysts.[22] So the cost of drones must not only include this enormous expense, but the trade-off of seconding thousands of the National Guard and other personnel.

The Congressional Budget Office in 2011 questioned the whole idea of 'cheap drones.' Their study remarked that the original concept was that these would be very low-cost, essentially expendable aircraft. 'As of 2011, however, whether substantially lower costs will be realized is unclear. Although a pilot may not be on board, the advanced sensors carried by unmanned aircraft systems are very expensive and cannot be viewed as expendable.'[23] The electro-optical/infrared cameras on small UAVs cost several times the drones themselves. And on the other end of the size spectrum, the sensors on the massive Global Hawk make up over half the vehicle's price tag. In general, as the technology becomes more and more sophisticated, the price of high-tech drones is expected to go up.

The Congressional study noted another big problem with drones that greatly affects the ultimate price tag. They crash—a lot. 'Excessively high losses of aircraft can negate cost advantages by requiring the services to purchase large numbers of replacement aircraft,' the report concluded.[24]

In 2009, the Air Force made an astonishing admission: more than a third of their unmanned Predator spy planes had crashed, mostly in Iraq and Afghanistan.[25] As of July 2010, 38 Predators and Reapers had been lost during combat operations in Afghanistan and Iraq, with another nine crashing during training operations in the US.[26] Altogether, the US Air Force said there had been seventy-nine drone accidents.[27]

A Predator crashed in the Afghan mountains in September 2010 after an oil system malfunction caused engine failure. A few months earlier, a crash was due to an electrical system failure. One disaster near Kandahar Air Base was attributed to a remote pilot pushing the wrong button. Another drone crashed just as it was landing in the Seychelles, the Indian Ocean nation where the US bases a fleet of drones. In the famous case of the Iranian government getting hold of the sophisticated US spy plane, the RQ-170, the Iranians claimed they brought down the plane by jamming its GPS, while the US claimed it was a 'technical problem' with the aircraft.

In an alarming preview of what is to come with drones clogging the airspace, in August 2012 a drone in Afghanistan collided with a C-130 cargo plane, forcing it to make an emergency landing. A spokesman for the US military in Afghanistan claimed that the C-130 received only light damage and that the aircrew was unharmed, but the incident raised grave concerns about the drone's inability to sense and avoid other aircraft.

In June 2012 the military's largest drone, the Global Hawk, did not crash in some far-flung overseas outpost but right here at home, in southern Maryland. The aircraft, valued at $176 million, was on a Navy test mission when the ground pilot lost control. Luckily, it crashed into a marsh, not a residential neighborhood.[28] And in March 2011, General Atomics' Grey Eagle went down in California when a faulty chip blocked a subsystem from sending commands to the aircraft's flight control surfaces.

Air Force investigators reported a variety of reasons

for all these crashes, including computer glitches, human error, coordination snafus, outdated technology and inadequate flight manuals. This was especially true during the first few years after 2001, they say, when drones were pushed into the air without adequate testing and training. But obviously, the problems persist.

Drones can also 'go rogue,' meaning that the remote control is no longer communicating with the drone. In 2009, the US Air Force had to shoot down one of its drones in Afghanistan when it went rogue with a payload of weapons. In 2008, an Israeli-made drone used by Irish peacekeepers in Chad went rogue. After losing communication, it decided on its own to start heading back to Ireland, thousands of miles away, and crashed en route.

The Navy's multimillion-dollar drone has the unfortunate feature of starting to self-destruct if the pilot accidentally presses the spacebar on his keyboard. As Fox News reported, 'An unmanned MQ-8B Fire Scout helicopter can launch by itself, fly by itself—and with a single slip, can nearly blow up by itself.'[29] According to a June 24, 2011 report from the Defense Department, a Navy pilot operating an unmanned helicopter accidentally pressed the spacebar with a wire from his headset. The crisis was averted at the last minute, but the Navy's MQ-8B has so many flaws that it failed ten of ten test missions at the Naval Air Station in southern Maryland. In fact, a glitch led one of the aircraft to fly uncontrolled from the station into restricted airspace near Washington, DC, before control was regained.[30]

Another problem with drone systems is security flaws.

Many Reapers and Predators didn't encrypt the video they transmitted to American troops on the ground. In the summer of 2009, US forces discovered 'days and days and hours and hours' of drone footage on the laptops of Iraqi militants. A $26 piece of software allowed them to capture the video.[31]

None of the remote cockpits are supposed to be connected to the public Internet, which means they should be largely immune to viruses and other network security threats. But time and time again, the so-called 'air gaps' between classified and public networks have been bridged, largely through the use of discs and removable drives.

In late 2008, for example, the drives helped introduce the agent.btz worm to hundreds of thousands of Defense Department computers. Three years later, the Pentagon was still disinfecting machines.

In September 2011, a computer virus infected the Creech computers, logging pilots' keystrokes as they remotely flew missions over Afghanistan and other war zones.[32] Military network security specialists weren't sure whether the virus was introduced intentionally or by accident. But they were sure that the infection hit both classified and unclassified machines at Creech, raising the possibility that secret data might have been captured and transmitted over the public Internet to someone outside the military chain of command.

Finally, there are also serious questions about exactly how precise the munitions dropped from these drones really are. Air Force Lt. Gen. David Deptula said that of more than 600 Hellfires fired by Predators, over 95 percent hit their targets, with the few failures attributed to mechanical fault, loss of guidance or a target moving at the last instant.[33] But others question this precision, citing the problem of 'latency,' the delay between movement on the ground and the arrival of the video image via satellite to the drone pilot. And if Hellfires are so accurate, one has to wonder why Lockheed Martin is being funded by Congress to upgrade the Hellfire to 'Romeo II,' which is supposed to have a better guidance system, maintenance and mechanisms for preventing systems failures. How precise can these 'precision munitions' be if they need so many improvements?

While much of the reporting on drone attacks is classified, it does seem that some of the problems of accuracy and reliability have to do with weather conditions. Clouds, rain, fog and smoke can reduce their accuracy. Then there are equipment errors and design defects, such as problems with laser targeting where some of the laser energy is reflected back from the target, confusing the laser seeker.

In order to compensate for these deficiencies, the Air Force developed a tactic called 'double tap,' firing two Hellfire missiles at each target. But this increases the possibility of more civilian deaths, as individuals who rush to help those who were hit from the first strike are themselves blown up with the second attack. A study by the UK-based Bureau of Investigative Journalism found evidence that at least fifty civilians were killed in follow-up strikes when they had gone to help victims.[34]

Even when missiles hit their designated target,

casualties and damage are not necessarily confined to the specific individual, vehicle, or structure targeted. The blast radius from a Hellfire missile can extend anywhere from 15 to 20 meters, and shrapnel may also be projected significant distances from the blast.

Of course, when the target is falsely identified, even the most accurate bombs will result in tragedy. From Afghanistan to Somalia, the US is operating in regions where it has a limited understanding of the intricacies of those complex societies. Faulty intelligence can be the product of deliberate misinformation from local informants who are trying to either settle old tribal feuds or simply make some cash by selling phony tips. Remember, on the basis of local tips, accompanied by bounty payments, the Bush administration rounded up close to 1,000 people and threw them in Guantanamo. Defense Secretary Donald Rumsfeld called them 'the worst of the worst'—and then 80 percent of them were found to be innocent. And after ten years in Afghanistan, with 100,000 boots on the ground, US soldiers were still confusing friend and foe.

Faulty intelligence can also be the product of simple mistakes. Despite all the super-duper cameras, video images can be misinterpreted. A truck carrying boxes of pomegranates can look just like a truck carrying boxes of explosives. A tall, bearded man in a robe can look just like another tall, bearded man in a robe. In February 2002, a drone pilot reportedly killed three Afghan men, including a tall Afghan who he thought was Osama bin Laden but turned out to be an innocent villager gathering scrap metal.[35] During the 2003 Iraq invasion, semi-automated

Patriot missiles were fired at what were supposed to be Iraqi rockets: the result was downed allied planes. Their human operators were supposed to override in such cases but failed to do so.[36]

And in the first known case of friendly fire deaths involving unmanned aircraft, a drone strike in Afghanistan on April 6, 2011 accidentally killed a US Marine and a Navy medic. Marine Staff Sgt. Jeremy Smith, 26, and Navy Hospitalman Benjamin D. Rast, 23, were killed by a Predator drone after Marine commanders mistook them for Taliban. When Jeremy Smith's father, Jerry Smith, was shown video images of the attack, he didn't see the high-resolution images one might expect from sophisticated drones. All he could make out were blobs in really dark shadows. 'You couldn't even tell they were human beings—just blobs,' said the bereaved father. The report found no one culpably negligent or derelict in their duties, but faulted poor communications, mistaken assumptions and 'a lack of overall common situational awareness.'[37]

Unfortunately, gravesites throughout Asia and the Middle East are filled with testaments to drone attacks gone bad. And drones are not named Predators and Reapers for nothing. They are killing machines. With no judge or jury, they obliterate lives in an instant, the lives of those deemed by someone, somewhere, to be terrorists, along with those who are accidentally—or incidentally—caught in their cross-hairs.

Think how terrifying it must be to live under the constant threat of a drone attack. Sometimes you'd see them flying menacingly overhead; sometimes they'd disappear but you could still hear their frightening, buzzing sound.

Drone attacks leave behind trails of human suffering—grieving widows, orphaned children, young lives snuffed out, lifetime disabilities. They enrage local populations, stoke anti-American feelings and prompt violent acts of revenge.

As Pakistani-American attorney Rafia Zakaria wrote, 'Somewhere in the United States, a drone operator sits in a booth with a joystick and commandeers a pilot-less aircraft armed with deadly bombs. Much like in a video game, he aims, shoots and fires at targets he sees on a satellite map.... Sometimes the target is killed and sometimes the intelligence is faulty and a sleeping family or a wedding party bears the brunt of the miscalculation. At all times, however, the Taliban capitalize on the ensuing mayhem and gain new recruits and re-energize old ones. Terror thus spreads not simply in the village where the drone attack has taken place but far and wide in the bazaars of Peshawar and the streets of Lahore and the offices of Islamabad where these recruits avenge their anger against the drone attacks.'[38]

And while lots of people are being killed by drones, a few people are making lots of money.

2

It's a Growth Market

'We have just won a war with a lot of heroes flying around in planes. The next war may be fought by airplanes with no men in them at all. Take everything you've learned about aviation in war, throw it out of the window, and let's go to work on tomorrow's aviation. It will be different from anything the world has ever seen.'

—General Hap Arnold, V-J Day, August 1945

The US manufacturing sector is struggling, if not quite dead yet. Thanks to tax breaks and misleadingly labeled 'free trade' agreements, corporations have been given every incentive to look abroad for cheaper sources of labor, eliminating middle-class jobs even as wealthy CEOs get wealthier. Large swaths of Detroit, once a bustling city home to the country's largest employers, now resemble a ghost town.

But there's one manufacturing sector that's not hurting: the companies that profit from building the high-tech tools of modern warfare, America's last great export. Indeed, what former President Dwight D. Eisenhower called the 'military-industrial complex' has made it through this age of austerity largely unscathed. And when it comes to drones, the complex is booming.

'It's a growth market,' crowed the Defense Department's chief weapons buyer, Ashton B. Carter.[39] And he should know, with the Pentagon's $5 billion war chest for drones. Global spending on the research and manufacture of drones is expected to total more than $94 billion between 2011–2020, according to one analyst who monitors the aerospace industry. Other countries, particularly Israel and China, will take a piece of the pie. But this is one area where, so far, US companies are still in the lead.

No company has benefited more from the drone boom than San Diego-based General Atomics. While not as well known as mega-military contractors like Lockheed Martin or Boeing, the company, which began in 1955 building nuclear reactors, has experienced massive growth from the military's increased reliance on UAVs. In fact, the company's Predator became the global face of the new age of robotic warfare. Its successor, the Reaper (originally called Predator B)—which can fly higher and faster and hold significantly more weapons—has become the Air Force's primary unmanned aerial vehicle.

General Atomics bought its way into the drone business in the 1990s, purchasing from Hughes Aircraft the original

UAV company started by Israeli engineer Abraham Karem. While it's a private company, General Atomics would go belly-up in no time if it weren't for a constant stream of government contracts. Of the company's $661.6 million in revenues in 2010—up from just $115 million in 1980—90 percent came directly from sales to the Pentagon.[40] Between 2000 and 2010, it sold more than $2.4 billion worth of equipment to the US military. Most of that income is from drones.

With the red-hot drone market, the company's revenues are set to explode even more. And General Atomics is ready.

As the *Los Angeles Times* reported, its seven buildings spread over a sprawling 85-acre base in Poway, California, are 'believed to be the world's largest facility dedicated to drones.'[41] General Atomics' employees, who number around 5,000 in total, are busy just trying to keep up with the demand, while also working on the next generation of killer unmanned vehicles. 'Donning bright-blue smocks, employees work around the clock, pounding sheets of metal into aircraft parts or fusing electronics onto circuit boards.'

From 1994 to 2012, the company sold more than 800 of its Predator, Reaper, and Grey Eagle drones to the US military. It also began sales to NATO allies.[42]

In 2011, the US Air Force ordered a test version of General Atomics' latest, most souped-up drone, the Predator C Avenger, which can fly faster (740 km/h), higher (60,000 ft) and carry a bigger payload (over 2,000 pounds) than either the Predator or the Reaper.[43]

How did such a small company come to beat out its larger competitors in the drone-making game, despite the fact that its early UAVs that were used in the Balkans were difficult to control and prone to crashing?

'For our size, we possess more significant political capital than you might think,' company CEO James Blue boasted to a trade publication back in 2005.[44]

That political capital did not come based solely on the merits of the products Blue's company makes. And it did not come cheap.

For years, General Atomics carefully cultivated key members of Congress, spending lavishly on campaign contributions and junkets. As the Center for Public Integrity reported in 2006, the company spent more than any other corporation in America on financing trips abroad for lawmakers, their families and their staff.[45] Between 2000 and mid-2005, it spent 'roughly $660,000 on 86 trips' to everywhere from Turkey to Australia, where the company was trying to get US government approval to sell its latest UAVs overseas to non-NATO countries.

'[It's] useful and very helpful, in fact, when you go down and talk to the government officials to have congressional people go along and discuss the capabilities of [the plane] with them,' explained Tom Cassidy, CEO of the company's drone-making subsidiary, General Atomics Aeronautical Systems. A former Navy Admiral himself, which no doubt helps when selling his merchandise, Cassidy formed General Atomics' drone-making subsidiary in 1992 with just a half-dozen engineers.

General Atomics wasn't looking just to sell to the US

military and NATO allies, but was pushing for government permission to sell to other US allies, including repressive Middle Eastern regimes. 'There's interest from Pakistan, Saudi Arabia, Egypt and the United Arab Emirates,' boasted Frank Pace, president of the company's aircraft systems subsidiary, according to the Bloomberg news service. 'Saudi Arabia is a huge country, and if they want to cover the country well, they alone could get 50 aircraft.'[46]

In July 2010, the US government approved an export version of its flagship Predator drone model to the Middle East and South Asia. Prior to this, the sale of Predators was approved only to NATO countries, Japan, Australia, and New Zealand. In theory, these export versions are designed only for surveillance and reconnaissance missions, but it wouldn't take much adjusting to slap a bomb on them.

It's also helpful to have US congressmen in your pocket in order to help sell your wares back home, of course. The office of disgraced former Congressman Randy 'Duke' Cunningham, a San Diego Republican convicted of accepting bribes from military contractors, accepted more than $53,000 in trips to Europe and Australia from General Atomics between 2002 and 2005, according to the Center for Public Integrity.

As chair of the powerful House sub-committee that appropriated military spending, Cunningham was a useful advocate for the firm, pressing then Defense Secretary Donald Rumsfeld in July 2001 to speed up funding for General Atomics' Predator drone. Since then, the company's revenues have skyrocketed, partly from a 2010 contract worth $195 million to build a drone for use by the Army and another $148.2 million contract in 2011 to provide another two dozen of its MQ-9 Reaper drones to the Air Force.

Overall, the company has spent more than $21 million lobbying public officials since 1998, according to the Center for Responsive Politics.[47] But by 2008 this little company made it into the *Defense News* list of top one hundred defense firms. One would be hard pressed to find such an enormous return on investment outside the military-industrial complex.

General Atomics is not the only little military contractor that could. While it may sound like a gentle air freshener—and it did start out consulting on air quality—AeroVironment has been gobbling up a giant-size piece of the drone pie.

Like General Atomics, the company is relatively small. In 2001, AeroVironment's annual revenue was under $30 million. Within a decade, its revenue shot up to nearly $300 million, 85 percent of that coming from the sale of drones to the US government.

Compared to the likes of Boeing and Lockheed Martin, this southern California (Simi Valley) company is still the little brother. Finding its niche in mini-drones, AeroVironment has gotten into UAVs in a big way.

On September 1, 2011, the company announced it was awarded a $4.9 million contract from the US Army to build a 5 ½ pound drone called the Switchblade. Like its namesake, the Switchblade is versatile. According to AeroVironment, it is designed to provide the warfighter with a 'magic bullet' capable of being launched from the air or the ground and to lock in on a target within minutes.

'The unique capabilities provided by the Switchblade agile munition for standoff engagement, accuracy and controlled effects make it an ideal weapon for today's fight and for US military forces of the future,' said Bill Nichols from the Army's Close Combat Weapons Systems office.

But Nichols left out the juiciest detail: the mini-drone can also serve as the US military's very own robotic suicide bomber. In the words of the *New York Times,* it is being designed not just to provide surveillance, but to 'carry an explosive payload into a target.'[48] In other words, the Switchblade is an unmanned kamikaze fighter, a technology the military frets 'will not long be beyond the capabilities of a terrorist network.'

Later in September 2011, AeroVironmnet received a $6.9 million order from the US Air Force for another drone, the Raven, which can fit inside a backpack, and another $16 million order from the Army to provide support for the Raven.[49] The next month it got another boost: a $7.3 million Army order for its larger, 13-pound surveillance Puma drone.[50]

AeroVironment's itsy-bitsy surveillance Hummingbird Drone was featured by *Time* magazine as one of the best inventions in 2011. Built as a prototype for the Defense Advanced Research Projects Agency, it can fly in all directions, even backward. It can hover and rotate clockwise or counterclockwise, and is equipped with a video camera. It's shockingly light—weighing less than one

AA battery—but carries, at least during the experimental phase, a shockingly hefty price tag of $4 million.

With the Hummingbird, Raven, Wasp, Puma and Switchblade, AeroVironment has established itself as the giant of the mini-drones.

But don't think the big guns of the defense industry have been left out. Take Raytheon, which boasts more than 12,000 employees and is one of the top five largest federal contractors in the United States. Raytheon provides the US military with drone software enabling it to attain 'real-time access to actionable intelligence' gathered by drones around the world.[51] That's the technology that helps a drone pilot in a Nevada desert decide when to fire a Hellfire missile. Since the system allows military personnel to gather intelligence from a range of drones manufactured by other companies, it gives Raytheon a chance to win even when it loses out on a UAV contract to a competitor.

Raytheon also produces a 500-pound bomb called the Paveway for use by larger drones like the Predator. It's developing a 100-pound missile called The Monsoon to challenge the dominant role of the 100-pound Hellfire made by competitor Lockheed Martin.

But Raytheon is discovering that smaller may be better, and is now developing lightweight drone bombs. The *Arizona Daily Star* in Tucson, where Raytheon's missile and drone building is headquartered, reported in 2010 that the company was 'quietly vying for a key role in America's remote-control war on insurgents and terrorists' by engineering smaller and smaller missiles.[52] It produced the Griffin, which weighs less than one-third of the 100-pound

Hellfire missile. By 2010, Raytheon had already received more than $40 million in contracts from the US Army for the Griffin.

Even smaller is the 13-pound, 2-foot-long Small Tactical Munition designed, in the words of program manager Cody Trestchok, to meet an 'emerging need' for missiles to be strapped onto smaller drones that have been, up until now, only used for surveillance.[53] Raytheon also designed its own Cobra drone to carry this little bomb.

Reporting on Raytheon's successful September 2011 test of the Cobra, *Wired*'s Spencer Ackerman remarked, 'The guided munition has the potential to expand the drone war dramatically, giving battalion-sized units that fly small drones the ability to kill people, like the remote pilots who fly the iconic Predators and Reapers do.'[54]

Raytheon is also producing a system designed to shoot down enemy drones with lasers. But Raytheon, the largest employer in all of southern Arizona, is not content just providing the software, missiles and lasers for other company's drones—and the ability to shoot them down. Indeed, the *Daily Star* reports it is busy at work on technology that would keep 'drones in the air indefinitely,' having received a patent 'for a system that would allow one unmanned aerial vehicle to communicate in order to safely refuel another drone in flight.'[55]

And keep an eye out for what *Popular Science* calls a 'Supersonic Shape-Shifting Bomber.' With a target completion date of 2020, a Raytheon unmanned bomber—also called Switchblade—will have adjustable wings that will purportedly enable it to 'loiter just outside enemy territory for more than a dozen hours and, on command, hurtle toward a target faster than the speed of sound.'

Raytheon better hurry up, as the market, and the sky, is getting increasingly crowded.

Chicago-based military contractor Boeing, with more than 165,000 employees and revenues of over $64.3 billion in 2010, is not content losing out on the lucrative drone business to the likes of Raytheon, much less a company a fraction of its size, like General Atomics. First flown in April 2011, Boeing's Phantom Ray prototype is roughly the size of a fighter jet. But unlike drones currently in widespread use, this one essentially flies itself.

'Autonomous, fighter-sized unmanned aircraft are real,' said program manager Craig Brown after the first test flight. 'The bar has been raised.'

According to the *Los Angeles Times*, the Phantom Ray differs from existing, weaponized drones in that it does not require a human pilot to do much more than chart a flight path.[56] It could 'carry out a mission controlled almost entirely by a computer.'

Though it currently has no buyer for the Phantom Ray, estimated to cost around $60 to $70 million, the company is confident it will, someday.

'The reason we're doing this, fundamentally, is to make sure the Boeing Company has a core competency in this area,' Darryl Davis, president of Boeing's Phantom Works research and development division, explained in 2009.[57] 'You want to be ahead of the market and not be reacting.'

But when it comes to building autonomous flying killer robots, Boeing's not alone. General Atomics already has a model, the Gray Eagle, which is currently deployed in Iraq. 'It thinks for itself,' gushed General Atomics executive James Bouchard in a company press release entitled, 'Armed and Dangerous—the Gray Eagle goes lethal.'[58]

You don't even have to be a certified pilot to fly it. 'The aircraft is very autonomous,' raved Capt. Mike Goodwin. 'It's the latest and greatest.'

But Boeing is in a class of its own when it comes to building a top-secret unmanned robotic aircraft designed to be launched into space. Its X-37B Orbital Test Vehicle was in development for ten years at Boeing's 'Phantom Works' shop, after NASA selected Boeing to design and develop the vehicle in 1999. NASA paid Boeing over $400 million for the spacecraft, which is capable of staying aloft for over 270 days. It was first launched from Cape Canaveral Air Force Station in Florida in April 2010, serving as a test platform for secret experiments, and landed 244 days later in Vandenberg Air Force Base in California. While details of the flight are classified, it was reported to be a successful test run, although the bumpy landing blew out the left main landing gear tire on touchdown, causing damage to the belly of the vehicle in about seven places.

Despite the enormous price tag, Boeing was contracted to build a second vehicle, which was launched in March 2011. Once again, the details of its mission were withheld from the public.

Northrop Grumman also jumped into the drone race. Its signature drone, the Global Hawk, became controversial for its huge cost overruns. It was originally part of a $12 billion Air Force program that aimed to replace the Air

Force's aging fleet of 1950s-era U-2 spy planes with modern UAVs. The military describes the Global Hawk as a 'high-altitude, long-endurance unmanned aircraft system,' one capable of surveilling large swaths of territory, as opposed to the more limited range of vision offered by smaller UAVs.[59] According to the *New York Times*, the unmanned Global Hawk surveillance plane is being manufactured at the company's factory in Palmdale, California. Notably, the factory employs 'just fifty people,' suggesting that investments in militarism are not the best way to create jobs during a global economic downturn.[60]

'The Global Hawk is a very impressive product,' industry analyst Richard Aboulafia told the *Times*, 'but it is also a very expensive product.' Since 2001, the cost of the Global Hawk program has more than doubled, as military programs are wont to do. Each plane is now expected to cost a whopping $218 million. By contrast, the largest armed drone, the Reaper, costs $28 million and the Predator about $4.5 million.

Investing $218 million in anything is a lot of money. But investing $218 million in a plane that 'Pentagon tests also suggested...was not reliable enough to provide sustained surveillance' is just plain foolish. It is also, unfortunately, typical for the Pentagon, which is accustomed to getting away with wasting taxpayer money with little to no consequences.

A comparison of the Predator/Reaper program shows just what a dud the Global Hawk is.[61] In April 2010, General Atomics' Predator/Reaper aircraft had passed the one million flight hours milestone, with more than four hundred aircraft produced and flying nearly 80,000 missions, mostly in combat. This is compared with about four Global Hawks in service and fewer than 2,000 combat missions.

'Once again, we have a system that has failed to meet effectiveness and suitability requirements, but one that no doubt will proceed post-haste into full production and deployment,' said Thomas P. Christie, a former Pentagon testing official.[62]

On the other hand, maybe not. Citing budget constraints, the Pentagon announced in January 2012 that it was changing its plans to replace its fleet of U-2 spy planes with the Global Hawk. A Defense Department official said the latter's massive cost had 'priced itself out of the niche, in terms of taking pictures in the air.'[63] Apparently, not even the $165,000,000 Northrop Grumman invested in bribing US officials from 1998–2011 could get the Pentagon to overlook the massive costs and problems with its flagship drone.[64] So much for UAVs being a cheap, efficient panacea for all the military's needs in the 21st century.

The giant Bethesda, Maryland-based military contractor Lockheed Martin, with more than 130,000 employees and 2010 sales upwards of $45.8 billion, has also been greasing the wheels[65] with $142,000,000 in lobbying (1998–2011)[66]—and reaping the benefits with three-quarters of its revenues coming from military sales.[67]

One gift that it keeps on giving is its Hellfire missiles, the weapon of choice that UAVs have been raining down from the sky at a handsome $68,000 a shot. Lockheed has developed an even more deadly version that it lovingly calls the Romeo Hellfire. Dripping with sexual innuendos, Lockheed brags that the Romeo can 'lock onto targets before or after launch,' 'engage targets to the side and behind them without maneuvering into position,' and thanks to its more virile guidance and navigation capabilities, can 'increase the missile's impact angle and enhancing lethality.'[68] Speaking about this man's man of missiles, managing editor Gareth Jennings from *Jane's Missiles and Rockets* gushed, 'Before you would have to employ a specific missile-type to take out a particular kind of target—tank, truck, foot soldier. This allows the aircraft to engage "targets of opportunity" as they appear on the battlefield.'[69]

Proving that size is not everything, Lockheed Martin is also getting into the drone business in smaller ways. It is developing a concept drone called the Samarai Monocopter, which the magazine *Popular Mechanics* reports is inspired by 'the winding flight of a falling maple seed.' This would almost be beautifully poetic were its purpose not to provide 'a powerful...tool for soldiers' on the battlefield.[70]

Lockheed's contribution to the new world of warfare doesn't stop there. Lockheed also makes its own surveillance UAVs at its so-called 'Skunk Works' facility in Palmdale, California. Chief among Lockheed's drones is the stealth RQ-170 Sentinel model primarily used by the US Air Force and better known because of its enormous size as the 'Beast of Kandahar.' Beyond acknowledging its massive, roughly 40-foot wingspan drone, the military has been characteristically tight-lipped about its role on the battlefield. But according to the *National Journal*'s Marc Ambinder, it was that very Lockheed Martin drone that provided surveillance for the Navy SEAL operation that ended in the execution of Al Qaeda leader Osama bin Laden.[71] Less exciting for the company is the fact that it was this very model that showed up on TV screens around the world, in the hands of the Iranian government.

What the big companies like Lockheed, Boeing and Northrop Grumman are bringing to the drone market, which General Atomics and other small companies can't do, is the ability to produce high-performance supersonic aircraft. This marks the transition from using drones against peasants in Afghanistan to turning them against military forces with heavy modern weapons, such as those of Iran, North Korea and China. According to robotics expert Mark Gubrud, 'What lurks behind this is the specter of drone-vs-drone warfare or possibly robotized military standoffs, where the potential exists for automated responses to initiate or rapidly escalate warfare between major powers and between nuclear-armed states.'[72] Get ready for a drone-eat-drone world—fed by your tax dollars.

In addition to all the government-dependent private sector work on drones, the US government is doing its own research and production.

At the Wright-Patterson Air Force Base in Dayton, Ohio, the military is working on so-called 'micro air vehicles,' or MAVs, which resemble and mimic small birds and larger insects. The British *Daily Mail* reports that government researchers hope this tiny vehicle will soon be able to 'find, track and target adversaries while operating in complex urban environments.'[73]

Work at the Dayton facility, which is part of the Air Force Research Laboratory, began in May 2010. After the May 27 ribbon-cutting ceremony of its 'fortress-like' facility, a report in a local trade journal noted that the Air Force is 'pressing for tiny aircraft that can flutter down a city street or slip through an open window to spy on or attack enemy targets.'[74] To achieve this goal, government scientists have an entire indoor flight test facility complete with 60 motion-capture cameras intended to mimic an urban environment.

The military hopes the cool, killer technology will attract a steady stream of scientists interested in careers fashioning deadly gadgets out of a James Bond movie.

'We don't view this as necessarily an [Air Force] asset,' Douglas Blake, deputy director of the Air Vehicles Directorate, told the *Daily Mail*. 'We view it as a community asset.'

Once upon a time, libraries and parks were seen as community assets. In the age of the war on terror, facilities aimed at developing the next generation of miniature drones are the new baseball fields.

The efforts to construct tiny drone aircraft build on earlier work by the ultra-secretive Defense Advanced Research Projects Agency (DARPA) on 'a whole host of cyborg critters,' notes the *Daily Mail*.[75] Founded in 1958 in response to the Soviet's 1957 Sputnik satellite launch, DARPA is the US Defense Department's 'primary innovation engine,' according to the agency, undertaking 'projects that are finite in duration but that create lasting revolutionary change.'[76] This is no idle bragging, given that DARPA is credited, unlike Al Gore, with creating the Internet.

To this end, DARPA often employs unique methods for developing the next generation of military hardware. Indeed, in March 2011 the agency launched a crowd-sourcing competition, 'UAVForge,' to actually design a small drone that is 'small and light enough to carry in a rucksack' and capable of perching somewhere, vulture-like, for at least two hours while transmitting video back to its operators.[77]

The person or group who designs the best performing drone wins $100,000, which is a relatively cheap way for the US government to develop its latest war gadget. Opening up drone design to the public also has the added benefit of normalizing drone warfare among the public. As DARPA's Jim McComick told the media, 'We seek to lower the threshold to entry for hobbyists and citizen scientists,' the objective being an 'exchange of ideas among a loosely connected international community united through common interests and inspired by innovation and creative thought.'

The way DARPA puts the outsourcing of drone research, you'd almost think they were starting a hippie commune. But the US military isn't terribly interested in peace, love, and understanding—and it has its eyes on creating more than just lightweight surveillance drones.

Take, for instance, the 'Vulture.' With solar panels covering its massive 400-foot wingspan, the Vulture will be able to stay in the air for 5 years at a time, turning in lazy circles above any area that needs constant observation. Its day and night cameras (each with a 600-mile reach) will send information back to ground bases. During the day, the Vulture will be powered by sunlight through its solar panels, and by batteries at night. As an added kick, it may be equipped with missiles for lethal strikes.[78]

The Air Force is currently developing a technology named the Gorgon Stare after the many-eyed monster from Greek mythology 'whose unblinking eyes turned to stone those who beheld them.' This technology promises to greatly expand the surveillance capability of the Reaper drones it uses in Afghanistan and other sites in the war on terror.

As the disconcerting name suggests, the Gorgon Stare is a $15-million-a-pop system that utilizes multiple infrared and conventional cameras that the Air Force claims will dramatically broaden the view that a drone on the battlefield will be capable of capturing.[79] Reportedly, the system will allow drones to monitor all movement within a four square kilometer zone, whereas surveillance technology as of 2010 only allowed for the monitoring of less than one square kilometer.

But there's a problem: the technology might not be all it is cracked up to be. According to a draft of an Air Force report obtained by *Wired* magazine, December 2010 tests of the Gorgon Stare technology, which was to have already been deployed on the battlefield in Afghanistan by that point, found it to be 'not operationally effective' nor 'operationally suitable.'[80]

You don't have to be a military expert to know that is bad. And you don't have to be a prophet to know that this bad news will probably not stop the military from sinking ever more US tax dollars into the project. Indeed, the Air Force responded to the *Wired* report by reaffirming its commitment to the Gorgon Stare because 'lives depend on the quality of the intelligence' it promises to produce.

This enormous focus on unmanned vehicles is expected to continue for the decade 2011–2020, with the US accounting for 77 percent of worldwide research and development and about 69 percent of the procurement dollars.[81]

That's not to say other countries aren't experiencing their own drone booms. Take Israel.

'We're trying to get to unmanned vehicles everywhere on the battlefield for each platoon in the field,' Lt. Col. Oren Berebbi, the head of the Israel Defense Forces' technology division, told the *Wall Street Journal* in 2010.[82] 'We can do more and more missions without putting a soldier at risk.'

Indeed, now is a great time to be making drones. Giora Katz, vice president of the Israel-based Rafael Advanced Defense Systems Ltd., told the *Journal* he expects that a full one-third of all Israeli military hardware will be unmanned by 2025, if not sooner. 'We are moving into the robotic era.'

And like their counterparts in America, Israeli drone manufacturers—the most prominent of which are Aeronautics Defense Systems, Elbit Systems, and Israel Aerospace Industries (IAI)—aren't just producing their wares for a domestic market. Israel's perpetual war economy and combat history, combined with its early use of UAVs dating back to the occupation of the Sinai in the 1970s, have provided it with a competitive export edge.

A top Israeli official gave three reasons for Israel's world leadership in drones: 'We have unbelievable people and innovation, combat experience that helps us understand what we need, and immediate operational use since we are always in a conflict which allows us to perfect our systems.'[83] The 'combat proven' aspect of Israeli technology is advertised by the Israeli military, the media, and arms firms. Elbit Systems' Hermes 450—sold to at least a dozen nations—is advertised as 'Operational in the Israel Defense Force,' a fact highlighted with a bright yellow 'BATTLE PROVEN' stamp on the front of its brochure.[84]

In 2009, the Israeli government inked a deal to sell $50 million worth of drones to Russia.[85] That agreement was immediately followed by talk of another deal, this one worth $100 million.[86] By 2011, the state-owned Israeli Aerospace Industries had delivered a dozen drones to Russia as part of a $400 million contract.[87]

As of 2011, Russia was also eager to get its hands on a massive, weaponized Israeli drone called the Heron. About the size of a Boeing 737, the Heron can stay in the air for almost an entire day before needing to be refueled.

Like any dealer, Israel started by giving Russia just a taste, and now it's hooked. And it's not the only one. 'Israel is the world's leading exporter of drones, with more than 1,000 sold in 42 countries,' noted Jacques Chemia, chief engineer at IAI's drone division, in 2011.[88]

Turkey uses Israeli-made drones to conduct surveillance operations against Kurds in northern Iraq. India has purchased lethal drones as part of its long-running arms race with neighboring Pakistan,[89] which just produced its very own domestically made armed drone.[90]

The British have been collaborating with the Israelis on the production of their long-awaited and much-delayed Watchkeeper drone, which is based on the Israeli Hermes 450 and is being developed by a jointly owned Israeli-UK company. Separately, the British government, along with the private firm BAE Systems, is developing the Mantis, a drone that flies autonomously (without a remote pilot) according to a pre-programmed flight. The Brits are also entering into a joint venture UAV project with France.

While Israel and the US are the leaders in drone technology, they may be surpassed before long. China surprised many Western officials when, as the *Wall Street Journal* reported, it unveiled no fewer than twenty-five different types of UAVs at a trade show in November 2010, just four years after it unveiled its first concept model.[91] 'China's apparent progress is likely to spur others, especially India and Japan, to accelerate their own UAV development or acquisition programs,' the *Journal* reported. A distant second to the US when it comes to global military spending, China has already produced two drones, the Pterodactyl and Sour Dragon, that respectively mimic the features of the weaponized Predator drone and its surveillance, U-2-like sibling, the Global Hawk.

Even lesser military powers are getting in the game. Indeed, Iran has already begun deploying its own reconnaissance drones—one was shot down in Iraq in 2009[92]—and weapons-ready models are in the works, if not already in the field.[93] An Iranian state news outlet reported in March 2011 that the Islamic Republic had designed an 'unmanned flying saucer' equipped with a pair of ten megapixel cameras for aerial surveillance purposes. And in October 2012 the Iranian government gleefully announced a new long-range drone that can fly 2,000 kilometers, certainly far enough to reach Tel Aviv.

The US gave a boost to Iran's drone program, albeit unwittingly, when an RQ-170 Sentinel was downed in December 2011 after crossing into Iran, reportedly as part of a joint CIA-military spying program. Just like that, the top-secret technology the US spent millions of dollars and many years developing fell into the hands of an official enemy.

'It's bad—they'll have everything,' one US official told the *Los Angeles Times*.[94] 'And the Chinese or the Russians will have it too.' The technology was so valuable that the Obama administration even considered launching an air strike or sending a special operations team into Iran to destroy the downed drone.[95] A year after capturing the drone, Iranian officials claimed they had already reverse-engineered it and were building a replica. Iran, Russia, and China can thank US taxpayers for the gift.

In South Africa, meanwhile, in September 2011 two companies—Paramount Group and Aerosud Holdings Ltd—unveiled 'a compact plane that they say merges the capabilities of a drone, an attack helicopter and surveillance aircraft,' according to the *Wall Street Journal*.[96]

In October 2012 the Colombian government reported that it was manufacturing its own unmanned aircrafts, radars and sensors, as part of a defense and military innovation strategy. 'We have decided to make incursions in this field of technological development, like other countries, including Israel,' said Deputy Defense Minister Yaneth Giha.[97]

Billions upon billions of dollars have been spent from America to Asia on machinery, software and workers whose only purpose is building a better flying death robot. The best research centers and universities are dependent on military contracts. But only when one considers the things that time and money have not gone to—health care, education, infrastructure—can the full costs of this militarism be realized. Instead of researching better solar technology or the next generation of pacemakers, many of the world's top scientists are instead devoting their energy to coming up with the latest and greatest unmanned killing machines.

Former President Eisenhower spoke to the debilitating cost of devoting money to war and the preparation for war in a 1953 speech that still hits hard these many years later. Addressing a group of newspaper editors, Eisenhower decried the tremendous waste of money and manpower going to develop things that, ideally, the country would never use.

'Every gun that is made, every warship launched, every rocket fired signifies, in the final sense, a theft from those who hunger and are not fed, those who are cold and are not clothed,' Eisenhower remarked. 'This world in arms is not spending money alone. It is spending the sweat of its laborers, the genius of its scientists, the hopes of its children.'

Right now, some of America's brightest scientists are busy crafting new weapons of war on behalf of the merchants of death. As Eisenhower asked, 'Is there no other way the world may live?'

3

Here a Drone, There a Drone, Everywhere a Drone

'There are just pieces of flesh lying around after a strike. You can't find bodies. So the locals pick up the flesh and curse America. They say that America is killing us inside our own country, inside our own homes, and only because we are Muslims.'

—Noor Behram, Pakistani photographer[98]

Drones came of age in the US war on terror, namely, during the war in Iraq. Ironically, that war was itself sold to the American public and the international community in part based on the alleged threat posed by drones—in the wrong hands.

In a February 5, 2003 presentation before the United Nations Security Council, then US Secretary of State Colin Powell sought to sell the coming war to a skeptical world by pointing to Iraq's alleged possession of weaponized drones that could be used to attack the West with chemical or biological agents. The claim was debunked almost the moment it was made—the drones were for reconnaissance purposes only—but the story served its purpose: only a lunatic wouldn't fear a madman armed with flying death robots, corporate media outlets declared.[99] The rest is blood-soaked history.

The war in Iraq provided the US military a platform for perfecting its own deadly drones. In 2003 and 2004, the Army flew UAVs about 1,500 hours a month, according to *USA Today*; by mid-2006, that number had risen to about 9,000 hours a month.[100] In the eyes of many—outside the studios of Fox and CNN, that is—the US, not Iraq, had become the madman armed with flying death robots.

From the hunter-killer Predators and Reapers to the surveillance Global Hawks to the smaller, cheaper Ravens, the Air Force couldn't get its hands on enough UAVs for the wars in Iraq and Afghanistan. 'The demand far exceeds all of the Defense Department's ability to provide these assets,' Air Force Lt. Col. Larry Gurgainous told an AP reporter in 2008.[101]

In Afghanistan, by 2010 the Air Force was flying at least twenty Predator drones over stretches of hostile Afghan territory each day, providing a daily dose of some five hundred hours of video.[102] Most drones were used for surveillance purposes. 'For example, every day we're analyzing imagery that includes the need to distinguish between normal agriculture and poppy production,' one military officer told the *Christian Science Monitor*.[103]

But they were also used to target low-level Taliban fighters in remote areas and to support US troops in firefights. According to Air Force figures, the number of strikes kept increasing every year, from seventy-four drones strikes in 2007 to 333 by 2012, when the war was supposed to start winding down. In 2012, the US military was launching more drone strikes—an average of thirty-three per month—than at any moment in the eleven years of the Afghan conflict.

In Iraq, spy drones were used for everything from protecting oil fields to tracking supposed insurgents to distinguishing between 'plastics production...and homemade explosives production.'[104] Lethal drones were sent to target government buildings in Baghdad and to kill militants firing upon US positions.[105] The US military in Iraq came to rely on drones even more as it began to draw down its troop presence in 2008. The Bush administration launched a record number of lethal strikes at around the same time President Bush's 'surge' was about to end and both US and Iraqi politicians were trying to figure out the best way to get American troops out of the country without losing face.

Drones also proved useful after the ostensible US 'withdrawal' from Iraq in December 2011. Mandated by the Status of Forces Agreement negotiated by the Bush administration, the withdrawal resulted in the vast majority of combat troops being removed from the country but left behind more than 11,000 State Department employees—and the world's largest embassy in Baghdad—as well as a private, 5,000-strong mercenary force to protect them. And a fleet of UAVs.

As the *New York Times* reported and President Obama acknowledged in January 2012, US surveillance drones continued to fly through Iraq's nominally sovereign airspace well after the last Americans were supposed to have left the country.[106] The excuse: protecting all the State Department staff the US was leaving behind to meddle in the country's affairs. And the kicker: the UAVs were being operated not by the military, but by the State Department itself, the arm of the US government that once upon a time was associated with diplomacy, not drones.

At the time its drone program was revealed, the State Department insisted its fleet of UAVs were solely for surveillance purposes and that none of them were armed or even capable of being weaponized. For their part, though, Iraqis were skeptical.

'We hear from time to time that drone aircraft have killed half a village in Pakistan and Afghanistan under the pretext of pursuing terrorists,' Iraqi businessman Hisham Mohammed Salah told the *Times*. 'Our fear is that will happen in Iraq under a different pretext.'

While the Air Force was busy hunting and killing in Afghanistan and Iraq, where the US was involved in larger wars involving ground troops, other agencies—even non-military ones—took the killer drones to places around the world like Pakistan, Yemen, the Philippines and Somalia where the United States was not officially at war. In just a decade, the US Air Force, the CIA, the Joint Special Operations Command (JSOC) and mercenary groups like Blackwater (currently giving itself the professorial name Academi) had built up a global network of bases to pilot, test, maintain, arm, and launch drones. Many parts of this program are veiled in secrecy, especially those run by the CIA and JSOC, so its full extent is hard to assess.

As of October 2011, the US government was operating no less than sixty drone bases at home and around the world, according to journalist Nick Turse, from remote regions of Afghanistan and Pakistan to Ethiopia, Djibouti, Uzbekistan, Qatar, Turkey, and the United Arab Emirates.[107] A *Washington Post* exposé of Obama's global apparatus for drone killing said the network included 'dozens of secret facilities, including two operational hubs on the East Coast, virtual Air Force cockpits in the Southwest, and clandestine bases in at least six countries on two continents.'[108]

The most extensive—and lethal—drone program outside a war zone is run by the CIA. Publicly, the CIA does not even acknowledge this program's existence. When the American Civil Liberties Union (ACLU) tried to get information about the CIA's drone killings, the agency argued—and the court agreed—that even the 'fact of the existence or non-existence' of such a program was classified. But the CIA's drone assassination squad has become, next to Israel's nuclear weapons arsenal, perhaps the world's worst-kept classified secret.

Indeed, in October 2010, while delivering an on-the-record address before an auditorium full of American soldiers stationed in Italy, Defense Secretary and former head of the CIA Leon Panetta even cracked a joke about the program.

'[O]bviously I have a helluva lot more weapons available to me in this job than I had at the CIA,' Panetta told the troops, according to the Associated Press.[109] 'Although the Predators aren't that bad.'

Later that same day, Panetta noted US troops had helped affect regime change in Libya using the Global Hawk surveillance drone and the Predator—a hunter/killer aircraft that, he said, 'I was very familiar with in my last job.'

Panetta was not reprimanded for disclosing top-secret classified information and joking about what many legal experts consider war crimes. In the warped imperial culture of Washington, DC, when a low-level soldier like Bradley Manning leaks classified information with the express intent of revealing to the world the existence of war crimes, he faces life in prison. Panetta's joking disclosure, like President Obama's own quip about murdering the Jonas Brothers band with Predator drones, draws a hearty laugh from the establishment, not an indictment.

Before September 11, the CIA, stung by past assassination scandals, only used drones for surveillance. The week before the 9/11 attack, CIA Director George

Tenet was quoted by counterterrorism advisors as saying that it would be a 'terrible mistake' for the CIA to 'fire a weapon like this.'[110] Post-9/11, everything changed. The agency asked for, and received from President Bush, a secret memorandum giving it the right to target Al Qaeda virtually anywhere in the world. With the green light to kill, the CIA began putting its drones to work.

Begun under Bush and expanded under Obama, the CIA's program is classified as covert and the agency refuses to disclose where it operates, who is in charge, how targets are selected and approved, or how many people have been killed. It insists that releasing any information would aid the enemy. When former UN Special Rapporteur Philip Alston tried to get basic questions answered—both from the Bush and Obama administrations—'they blew me off,' he said.[111]

The CIA's main focus has been in Pakistan, where its missile strikes target suspected Al Qaeda operatives, as well as low-ranking militants believed to be involved in cross-border attacks on US troops or facilities in Afghanistan.

According to the Bureau of Investigative Journalism, between 2004–2012, the CIA conducted over 350 drone strikes in Pakistan, with a spike of 118 attacks in 2010, killing somewhere between 2,600 and 3,400 people. The CIA killing spree was so out of control that, according to the *New York Times*, State Department officials joked that when the CIA sees 'three guys doing jumping jacks,' the agency thinks it's a terrorist training camp and sends in the drones.[112]

At the end of 2011 the CIA suspended its missile strikes in an effort to mend badly frayed relations between the US and Pakistani government after US gunships mistakenly killed twenty-four Pakistani soldiers in November 2011. When the strikes resumed in mid-January 2012, against the wishes of the Pakistani government and people, Pakistani intelligence officials said the drone attacks were on the verge of pushing strained ties between the two nations to the point of collapse.

The CIA's partner, the military's Joint Special Operations Command (JSOC) is even more cloaked in secrecy and less subject to accountability than the intelligence agency. Founded in 1980, JSOC specializes in secret, small-scale operations. Since 9/11 its primary mission has been to identify and destroy perceived terrorists and terror cells worldwide. It is credited as the group that oversaw the raid that killed Osama bin Laden. In addition to dispatching clandestine troops, it has a drone hit team that it operates with the help of contracted mercenaries. It has carried out deadly strikes in Yemen and Somalia, but like the CIA, it refuses to disclose any aspect of its counterterrorism operations.

JSOC reports directly to the president and, as *National Journal* reporter Marc Ambinder put it, 'operates worldwide based on the legal (or extra-legal) premises of classified presidential directive.'[113] John Nagl, a former counterinsurgency adviser to Gen. Petraeus, described JSOC's kill/capture campaign as 'an almost industrial-scale counterterrorism killing machine.'[114]

JSOC targets come from a secret list called JPEL (Joint

Prioritized Effects List). According to Matthew Hoh, a former Marine and Foreign Service officer who resigned in 2009 because he felt US tactics were only fueling the insurgency, the list includes bomb makers, commanders, financiers, people who coordinate the weapons transport and even PR people.[115]

Another key partner in drone warfare are private contractors. 'From a secret division at its North Carolina headquarters, the company formerly known as Blackwater has assumed a role in Washington's most important counterterrorism program: the use of remotely piloted drones to kill Al Qaeda's leaders,' the *New York Times* reported in August 2009.[116] 'The division's operations are carried out at hidden bases in Pakistan and Afghanistan, where the company's contractors assemble and load Hellfire missiles and 500-pound laser-guided bombs on remotely piloted Predator aircraft, work previously performed by employees of the [CIA].'

A few months after the *Times'* story, *The Nation*'s Jeremy Scahill revealed that the relationship between Blackwater and the US government's covert drone assassination program ran even deeper. He reported that the company was intimately involved in the drone program run not just by the CIA, but by the military's ultra-secretive JSOC.

'It's Blackwater running the program for both CIA and JSOC,' Scahill quoted a source within US military intelligence as saying. According to the source, while many reported drone strikes in Pakistan are credited to the CIA, it is the parallel Blackwater-JSOC program that is responsible for the bulk of civilian casualties.

When civilians are killed, Scahill's source said, 'people go, "Oh, it's the CIA doing crazy shit again unchecked." Well, at least 50 percent of the time, that's JSOC [hitting] somebody they've identified through HUMINT [human intelligence] or they've culled the intelligence themselves or it's been shared with them and they take that person out and that's how it works.'

While the CIA is not exactly renowned for its respect for the lives of foreigners, the Blackwater-JSOC drone program is supposedly even more cavalier about killing civilians, as it is even less subject to congressional oversight.

'Targeted killings are not the most popular thing in town right now and the CIA knows that,' the source said, according to Scahill. 'Contractors and especially JSOC personnel working under a classified mandate are not [overseen by Congress], so they just don't care. If there's one person they're going after and there's thirty-four people in the building, thirty-five people are going to die. That's the mentality.'

In Yemen, both the CIA and JSOC are engaged in a covert bombing campaign aimed at taking out suspected members of Al Qaeda in the Arabian Peninsula. Both have their own flying hit teams, with separate but overlapping targets. Unlike in Pakistan, where the CIA has presidential authorization to launch strikes at will, each strike in Yemen requires White House approval and intended targets are drawn from an approved list of militants deemed by US intelligence officials to be involved in planning attacks against the West.[117]

In November 2002 the CIA conducted its first drone

strike in Yemen, killing Al Qaeda leader Abu Ali Al-Harithi, a suspect in the 2000 bombing of the USS *Cole*, and five others. This was the first and last drone attack under the Bush administration. Attacks really began in earnest under Barack Obama. In 2012 alone, Obama authorized around thirty drone strikes.

A drone strike in May 2010 mistakenly killed a key mediator between the Yemeni government and Al Qaeda in the Arabian Peninsula, Jaber al-Shabwani, the deputy governor of Maarib. He was killed while conferring with an Al Qaeda leader in an attempt to negotiate a settlement with the government. Also killed in the attack were three of his bodyguards and two operatives with Al Qaeda in the Arabian Peninsula.[118]

The Yemeni government apologized for Shabwani's death but the killing prompted members of his tribe to strike at government facilities, including a military camp, an oil pipeline, and power lines.[119] On January 30, 2012, a drone strike in southern Yemen killed at least twelve alleged Al Qaeda militants, including four local leaders.

The most high-profile attack in Yemen was in September 2011, when the CIA used a Predator drone to assassinate two US citizens, Anwar al-Awlaki and Samir Khan, alleged propagandists for a Yemeni terrorist organization inspired by Al Qaeda.[120] This was the seccond time the US government launched a drone strike against US citizens it considered terrorists. The first was on November 3, 2002, when a drone attack killed six terrorist suspects in Yemen, including US citizen Kemal Darwish, a key suspect in the Lackawanna terrorist plot in upstate New York. (The main target in that attack, however, was not Darwish but Qa'id Salim al-Harithi, a suspect in the lethal attack on the USS *Cole*.) Less than a month later, Awlaki's sixteen-year-old son, Abdulrahman, was also killed in a drone strike.[121]

Ironically, the CIA is forbidden under US law from spying on Americans—that's left to the FBI. It seems that the agency can, however, murder Americans overseas at the behest of the president without so much as a whimper of 'impeachment.'

According to a State Department cable released by the whistle-blowing website WikiLeaks, the bombings in Yemen were conducted with the approval of the long-time dictator of Yemen, Ali Abdullah Saleh, who in January 2010 reassured US officials that he would 'continue saying the bombs are ours, not yours.'[122] That promise is credited as one of the reasons the Yemeni people rose up against Saleh's repressive regime in 2011, despite the specter of frequently violent and bloody crackdowns, and forced him to leave the country in January 2012.

The drone war in Yemen is implicating another very dicey part of the world, Saudi Arabia. In the summer of 2011, it was reported that the deadly drones flying over Yemen's skies were coming from bases in the Arabian Peninsula,[123] which a senior US military official said means Saudi Arabia.[124] You might recall that none other than former Deputy Defense Secretary Paul Wolfowitz said the presence of US forces in Saudi Arabia had proven to be a 'huge recruiting device for Al Qaeda' and in fact one of the principal grievances of Osama bin Laden.[125]

Elsewhere in the Gulf, the US has reportedly been

flying UAVs from Kuwait and Oman, and running a support facility for its drone wars from an air base in Qatar.[126] According to Global Security, the Global Hawk has operated from the United Arab Emirates (UAE) since the early days of the invasion of Iraq, using the Al Dhafra Air Base outside the capital Abu Dhabi.[127] The move came despite the fact that Islamic groups in the UAE are critical of the government's close ties to the United States.

Across the Arabian Sea in Somalia, the *Washington Post* reported in September 2011 that the Obama administration has been flying drones over this war-torn, famine-ravished nation from a base in the tiny northeast African nation of Djibouti as part of its efforts to fight the Islamic insurgent group Al Shabab.[128]

Djibouti is a tiny, poor former French colony with less than one million people. The US military has had a presence in Djibouti since 2001 as a base for US operations in the Horn of Africa. Starting with a 2002 strike in Yemen that killed a suspected ringleader of the attack on the USS *Cole*, for a decade the United States flew an occasional drone from its base there called Camp Lemonnier. That changed dramatically in 2010, however, after Al Qaeda's network in Yemen attempted to bomb two US-bound airliners and jihadists in Somalia gained a foothold on that country. The Pentagon sent eight unmanned Predator drones to Djibouti and turned Camp Lemonnier into a full-time drone base. Sandwiched between East Africa and the Arabian Peninsula, this tiny remote nation provides a perfect location for US aircraft to reach hot spots such as Yemen or Somalia in minutes.

Clandestinely, the US military has transformed this into the busiest Predator drone base outside the Afghan war. 'Around the clock, about 16 times a day, drones take off or land at a US military base here, the combat hub for the Obama administration's counterterrorism wars in the Horn of Africa and the Middle East,' the *Washington Post* reported in October 2012.[129]

In October 2011, White House Press Secretary Jay Carney also confirmed that the US was flying drones out of a 'facility in Ethiopia as part of our partnership with the government of Ethiopia to promote stability in the Horn of Africa.'[130] According to Carney, the drones are not weaponized, but are 'unarmed reconnaissance aircraft' intended to be used as part of a 'broad, sustained and integrated campaign to counter terrorism.'

Not to worry, though: while armed drones were reportedly not yet based in Ethiopia, the *Washington Post* and *Wall Street Journal* reported in the fall of 2011 that the US was operating unmanned aircraft at a base in the island nation of Seychelles, an archipelago located off the coast of East Africa, and was considering weaponizing them.[131]

US and Seychelles officials originally said that the primary mission of the drones was to track pirates in regional waters. But classified US diplomatic cables showed that the plan was also to conduct counterterrorism missions over Somalia, about eight hundred miles to the northwest.[132]

The cables, obtained by WikiLeaks, revealed that US officials asked leaders in the Seychelles to keep the counterterrorism missions secret, something the president of the Seychelles was more than happy to do. A US military spokesman refused, on security grounds, to tell the *Washington Post* if the Reapers in the Seychelles have ever been armed but noted that they 'can be configured for both surveillance and strike.'[133]

According to the BBC in June 2011, the US expanded its reach even further into Africa by sending four drones to Uganda and Burundi.[134]

This constellation of bases for drones in Africa and the Arabian Peninsula was designed to create overlapping circles of surveillance in a region where the CIA thought Al Qaeda offshoots could continue to emerge.

Drones were also used in Libya, with 145 drone strikes launched in just the first six months of the 2011 effort to overthrow the regime of Muammar Qaddafi—a military operation which the Obama administration denied was even a real war.[135]

With most American troops leaving Iraq at the end of 2011, the US government made a deal with Turkey to fly Predator drones from the Turkish-US joint air base at Incirlik as part of a joint counterterrorism operation in northern Iraq.[136] Since 1984, the Turkish government has been fighting a separatist campaign by rebels of the outlawed Kurdistan Worker's Party, or PKK, which has militants based in northern Iraq. The drone deal with Turkey puts the United States squarely in the middle of not only the Turkey–Kurd conflict, but also a conflict between Turkey and Iraq.

And if you thought the withdrawal of US troops from Iraq and the pending withdrawal from Afghanistan would mean that these countries would be free of US drones, think again. According to the *Unmanned Daily News*, 'Though the US plans to withdraw completely from its two wars over the next several years, US UAVs will have a presence over Iraq and Afghanistan for decades to come.'[137]

But the overwhelming US dominance in the use of drones is coming to an end. By 2011, American officials were already publicly fretting that the technology they have spent decades and billions of dollars developing is beginning to fall into the hands of other nations, friends and foes alike.

'From Desert Storm to the present, the US and its allies have had relatively exclusive access to sophisticated precision-strike technologies,' Deputy Secretary of Defense William J. Lynn III remarked at a June 2011 conference in Washington on the future of war.[138] Over the next decade or two, he said, 'that technology will be increasingly possessed by other nations... thereby creating challenges for our ability to project power to distant parts of the globe.'

Indeed, Philip Alston, former UN Special Rapporteur on extrajudicial, summary or arbitrary executions, noted that an arms race spurred by the widespread use of unmanned aerial vehicles by the US government to assassinate its perceived enemies is already well under way. Between 2005 and 2012, the number of countries that acquired drones nearly doubled from about forty to more than seventy-five.[139] Most of these are for intelligence, surveillance, and reconnaissance missions, but many countries—including Israel, Russia, Turkey, China, India, Iran, the United Kingdom, and France—either have or are seeking weaponized drones.

Not content to just buy drones, many nations want to develop their own. A US government study found that over fifty countries were developing more than 900 different UAV systems. 'This growth is attributed to countries seeing the success of the United States with UAVs in Iraq and Afghanistan and deciding to invest resources into UAV development to compete economically and militarily in this emerging area,' the study reported.[140]

Some of these countries do not just possess the technology; they are already using it.

During its 2008-2009 invasion of the Gaza Strip known as 'Operation Cast Lead,' the Israeli Defense Forces repeatedly deployed unmanned aircraft to fire on suspected members of Hamas, the elected Palestinian government.

According to a leaked US State Department cable reported on by the Israeli newspaper *Haaretz*, in one incident an Israeli drone 'shot at two Hamas fighters in front of the mosque and sixteen unintended casualties resulted inside the mosque due to an open door through which shrapnel entered during a time of prayer.'[141] While the technology may be precise, fallible human beings are still the ones picking the targets and pulling the trigger.

Israel ostensibly ended its military occupation of the Gaza Strip in 2005. But thanks to modern drone technology, it does not need boots on the ground to dominate—and extinguish—Palestinian life.

'For us, drones mean death,' said Hamdi Shaqqura of the Palestinian Center for Human Rights in an interview with the *Washington Post*.[142] According to his group, Israeli drones killed at least 825 people between 2006 and 2011, the majority civilians. And that has affected almost every aspect of Palestinian life. According to one study, the majority of children living in Gaza suffer from post-traumatic stress disorder (PTSD) as a result of the constant buzzing and bombing of Israeli death machines. Palestinians even have to take drones into account when trying to do something as benign and banal as fixing a broken-down car—you really don't want a group of people lingering around for long when there's a plane armed with missiles hovering overhead. 'When you hear drones,' Shaqqura explained, 'you hear death.'

'It's continuous, watching us, especially at night,' said Nabil al-Amassi, a Gaza mechanic and father of eight. 'You can't sleep. You can't watch television. It frightens the kids. When they hear it, they say, "It is going to hit us."'

Along with Israel and the United States, Britain is the only other country to have employed weaponized drones in war as of 2011. In the 1980s, the UK developed the Phoenix, a drone that was briefly used in the Kosovo War and then in Iraq in 2003. So many were lost or crashed that British troops nicknamed the aircraft the 'Bugger Off,' as the planes rarely returned from a sortie.[143] For Afghanistan, the UK bought US-made Reapers and rented Israeli Hermes drones. This was part of a stopgap measure while developing their own Watchkeeper drone in a joint venture by Israeli and UK private companies that, after many delays, was supposed to be operational by 2012.[144]

Like their US and Israeli counterparts, the British government sees unmanned aircraft as the way of the future, with the *Guardian* reporting that UK officials say 'almost one third of the [Royal Air Force] could be made up of remotely controlled aircraft within 20 years.'[145]

In July 2011, British drone operators made a mistake that underscores the continued fallibility of modern weapons, killing four civilians in Afghanistan with missiles fired from Reaper drones that they were piloting out of a US air base in Nevada. (The Royal Air Force has been piloting Reapers from Creech Air Force base in Nevada since late 2007.) Lest anyone believe the incident exposed flaws with the increased reliance on the almighty drone, UK military officials were quick to explain the deaths were the result of intelligence failures on the ground rather than problems with the aircraft.[146]

That fallible human element does not harm just those on the receiving end of the West's liberating Hellfire missiles. When Iraqis were actually able to see the unencrypted video feeds that the unmanned vehicles were broadcasting back to US troops, it gave them the chance to escape and evade assassination.[147] In 2002, Iraqis were also able to use a Soviet-era MIG-25 to shoot down a US drone. In 2006, the Syrian air force reportedly shot down an Israeli spy drone flying on the Lebanese side of the border with Syria.[148] And in a little-reported incident in February 2011, as Yemeni police were transporting a Predator drone that had crashed in southern Yemen, Al Qaeda gunmen attacked, running off with the downed aircraft.

But the perceived enemies of the US government are doing more than just hijacking and shooting down drones: they are using their own.

During its 2006 war on Lebanon, the Israeli Defense Forces claimed to have shot down several surveillance drones that Hezbollah had received from Iran. This happened again in October 2012, when an Iranian drone launched by Hezbollah flew in Israeli airspace for three hours, beaming back live images of secret Israeli military bases, before being shot down by the Israeli military. In Iraq, US troops shot down a similar Iranian drone in March 2009.[149]

A 2012 study by the US Government Accountability Office found that because some types of drones are relatively inexpensive and have short development cycles, 'they offer even less wealthy countries a cost-effective way of obtaining new or improved military capabilities that can pose risks to the United States and its allies.' It reported that 'certain terrorist organizations' have acquired or are developing some form of drone technology. While it said that these organizations are currently limited to using smaller, more rudimentary UAVs—such as radio-controlled aircraft that are available worldwide from hobby shops or through the Internet—and that no terrorist organization has yet successfully carried out a drone attack, if terrorists were able to equip drones with even a small quantity of chemical or biological weapons, it could produce lethal results.[150]

Just as US drone technology is falling into less-than-friendly hands, the technology—like the Hummer and other military equipment before it—is finding its way back to the homeland. In a September 27, 2011 presentation at the headquarters of the US Air Force on the future of 'remotely piloted aircraft,' the branch's chief scientist Mark T. Maybury pointed to 'homeland security' as a key future use of drones, complete with maps of the United States intended to highlight the need for 'Integrating [drones] in National Airspace.'[151]

The future is here.

In 2005, Congress authorized Customs and Border Protection (CBP) to buy unarmed Predators. By the end of 2011, CBP was flying eight Predator drones along the southwestern border with Mexico and along the northern Canadian border to search for illegal immigrants and smugglers. By 2016, CBP hopes to have two dozen drones in its possession, 'giving the agency the ability to deploy a drone anywhere over the continental United States within three hours,' according to the *Washington Post*.[152] And beyond, it seems, as the US Drug Enforcement Agency (DEA) has deployed several drones in neighboring Mexico to spy on that country's powerful drug cartels.[153]

In June 2011, the *Post* reported that CBP's drone fleet had 'reached a milestone...having flown 10,000 hours.' But they had little to show for it. The paper flatly noted that the 4,835 undocumented immigrants and 238 drug smugglers that the Department of Homeland Security claimed to have apprehended thanks to UAVs were 'not very impressive' numbers. What is impressive is the cost: $7,054 for each undocumented immigrant or smuggler who was caught.

'Congress and the taxpayers ought to demand some kind of real cost-benefit analysis of drones,' said Tom Barry of the Center for International Policy, a Washington think tank. 'My sense is that they would conclude these aircraft aren't worth the money.'

But politicians in Washington don't seem too concerned. CBP's Michael Kostelnik told the *Post* he has never been pressed by a lawmaker to justify his agency's use of drones. 'Instead the question is: Why can't we have more of them in my district?'

Indeed, many lawmakers are cheerleaders for the drone industry, setting up their own Congressional Drone Caucus (formally known as the Unmanned Systems Caucus) specifically to lobby for more and better drones, to lift export restrictions, and to relax regulations by the Federal Aviation Administration (FAA) that limit the use of drones domestically.[154]

The FAA is responsible for the safety of the nation's airspace, and that's why any entity wishing to operate a UAV domestically must obtain FAA permission. The agency had been proceeding very cautiously out of concern that many of the remotely piloted aircraft don't have adequate 'detect sense and avoid' technology to prevent midair collisions. By 2012 it had only permitted a small number of domestic law enforcement agencies to use drones, with strict conditions attached.

But the FAA came under increasing pressure from Congress, industry, and law enforcement agencies to open the skies to UAVs. On February 14, 2012, President Obama gave a Valentine's Day present to the drone manufacturers.

He signed a $63.4 billion Federal Aviation Administration reauthorization bill that requires the FAA to come up with a comprehensive integration plan within nine months and to fully integrate drones into US airspace by September 15, 2015. The bill also requires expedited access for public users, like law enforcement, firefighters and emergency responders. Within ninety days, it must allow them to fly drones under 4.4 pounds, as long as they are kept under an altitude of 400 feet and meet other requirements.

The US drone lobby group that helped draft the bill, the Association of Unmanned Vehicle Systems International (AUVSI), was delighted; commercial airlines and pilots were not. They worry that the quick push to integrate drones will not only take away jobs, but lead to accidents. 'Until unmanned aircraft can show they won't run into other planes or the ground, they shouldn't be allowed to fly with other traffic,' said Lee Moak, president of the Air Line Pilots Association.[155]

Even before the new rules had gone into effect, the CBP had made some very unconventional—and some would say illegal—uses of its drones to assist local, state and federal law enforcement. As the *Los Angeles Times* reported in December 2011, CBP's Kostelnik acknowledged that far beyond just providing surveillance at the border, Predators are flown 'in many areas around the country, not only for federal operators, but also for state and local law enforcement and emergency responders in times of crisis.'[156]

It was deemed a crisis, I suppose, when drones were called in to Nelson County, North Dakota to help Sheriff

Kelly Janke look for six missing cows on the Brossart family farm in the early evening of June 23, 2011. The heroic drones helped find and apprehend the cattle rustlers—and rescue the six cows.

Police forces, full of veterans from Iraq and Afghanistan, are chomping at the bit to get the latest in 21st century military equipment. And while they anxiously await FAA approval, some departments have applied for—and received—permission to test out various kinds of drones.

The Miami-Dade Police Department in Florida purchased a 20-pound drone.[157] 'It gives us a good opportunity to have an eye up there,' Miami-Dade Police Director James Loftus told reporters. 'Not a surveilling eye, not a spying eye. Let's make the distinction. A surveilling eye to help us to do the things we need to do, honestly, to keep people safe.'

In November 2011, the Miami police department also obtained approval from the FAA to fly two $50,000-a-piece surveillance drones said to resemble flying garbage cans, albeit limited to heights of just three hundred feet.[158] 'No other law enforcement agency in the country is using this,' bragged Sergeant Andrew Cohen. 'We're forging new ground.'[159]

The Mesa County, Colorado, Sheriff's Office is testing a remotely operated miniature helicopter designed to carry wireless video, still cameras, and light thermal imaging equipment. The sheriff's office is using the testing process to gather information that could eventually lead to the helicopter being approved by the FAA for daily use by law enforcement for search and rescue operations, for providing real-time updates to tactical teams during crisis, or for simply sending the helicopter out to photograph a crime scene.

In October 2011, a police department just outside of Houston, Texas, dropped $300,000 in federal homeland security grant money on an unmanned, 50-pound helicopter decked out with a powerful zoom camera and infra-red equipment. While unarmed—for now—Michael Buscher, CEO of manufacturer Vanguard Defense Industries, told reporters the drone is designed to be weaponized and could in the future be outfitted with 'what we call less lethal systems.' Those include Tasers that can electrocute suspects on the ground and bean-bag-firing guns called stun batons.[160]

'You have a stun baton where you can actually engage somebody at altitude with the aircraft,' Buscher explained. 'A stun baton would essentially disable a suspect.' But not to worry, Sheriff Tommy Gage assured reporters. 'We're not going to use it to be invading somebody's privacy. It'll be used for situations we have with criminals,' he said. Situations, like hunting fleeing suspects. Or helping SWAT teams scope out an area during a standoff. Or during other criminal investigations, like those involving potential drug shipments.

Randy McDaniel, chief deputy with the Montgomery County Sheriff's Office, said their 50-pound ShadowHawk helicopter drone could be equipped with a 40-mm grenade launcher and a 12-gauge shotgun, and that they may decide to adapt it to fire tear-gas canisters and rubber bullets.[161]

A September 2012 Congressional Research Report

found that domestically, drones can be outfitted with high-powered cameras, thermal imaging devices, license plate readers, and laser radar (LADAR). 'In the near future, law enforcement organizations might seek to outfit drones with facial recognition or soft biometric recognition, which can recognize and track individuals based on attributes such as height, age, gender, and skin color...and will soon have the capacity to see through walls and ceilings,' the report stated.[162]

Feeling nervous? The ACLU is. The civil rights watchdog is particularly concerned that drones are moving us closer to a 'surveillance society' in which our every move is monitored, tracked, recorded, and scrutinized by the authorities. In a December 2011 report on aerial surveillance, the ACLU predicted that 'all the pieces appear to be lining up for the eventual introduction of routine aerial surveillance in American life—a development that would profoundly change the character of public life in the United States.' This is especially worrisome since 'our privacy laws are not strong enough to ensure that the new technology will be used responsibly and consistently with democratic values.'[163] The report concluded that based on current trends—technology development, law enforcement interest, political and industry pressure, and the lack of legal safeguards—'it is clear that drones pose a looming threat to Americans' privacy.'[164]

'The potential for abuse is vast,' warns constitutional lawyer and writer Glenn Greenwald. 'The escalation in surveillance they ensure is substantial, and the effect they have on the culture of personal privacy—having the state employ hovering, high-tech, stealth video cameras that invade homes and other private spaces—is simply creepy.'[165]

Equally creepy is the possibility that drone technology is not just coming back to the US by way of local law enforcement agencies desperate for new, Department of Homeland Security-funded gadgets. Soon, the technology could be brought back to the homeland whether US policymakers like it or not.

As Ralph Nader observed in a column published in the fall of 2011, drone technology is 'becoming so dominant and so beyond any restraining framework of law or ethics that its use by the US government around the world may invite a horrific blowback.'[166] Two days after the piece was published, a twenty-six-year-old man from Massachusetts, Rezwan Ferdaus, was arrested and accused of plotting to attack the Pentagon and US Capitol with small drone aircraft filled with explosives.[167] The plan he delivered to undercover agents involved using three remote-controlled planes, similar to military drones, guided by GPS equipment.

Ferdaus, a Northeastern University graduate with a degree in physics, had already used his skills to convert eight cell phones into detonators, supplying them to undercover agents who he thought were affiliated with Al Qaeda. FBI agents seemed to have egged him on to go further, providing him with assault rifles, grenades, 25 pounds of C-4 plastic explosives and even an F-86 remote-controlled aircraft.

According to the criminal complaint filed in court, the

planes were large enough to carry 'a variety of payloads (including a lethal payload of explosives), could use a wide range of take-off and landing environments, and could fly different flight patterns than commercial airlines, thus reducing detection.' The Capitol's dome would be 'blown to smithereens,' Ferdaus was quoted in the complaint as saying.

If he had succeeded in creating and launching a suicide-bombing drone, Ferdaus would arguably only have beaten the US government at its own game. Less than a month before news of the alleged plot was made public, the US Army announced it was awarding military contractor AeroVironment a $4.9 million contract to supply it with a small, backpack-size drone capable of crash-diving into a target kamikaze-style.[168]

John Villasenor, a professor of electrical engineering at the University of California, Los Angeles, told the *New York Times* such a drone in the hands of terrorists could pose a challenge that may prove extremely difficult to thwart. 'If they are skimming over rooftops and trees,' he said, 'they will be almost impossible to shoot down.'

Of course, for years so-called terror experts have warned of extremists setting off suitcase bombs in American cities. Despite the constant fear-mongering from the political establishment, the truth is that people in the Middle East have more to fear from the US government's weapons of war than the American public does from deadly tools in the hands of terrorists.

Still, while Ferdaus's plot was foiled and previous threats may have been overblown, the point was driven home: Watch out, America—what goes around, comes around.

4

Pilots without a Cockpit

'Death, destruction, disease, horror. That's what war is all about, Anon. That's what makes it a thing to be avoided. You've made it neat and painless. So neat and painless, you've had no reason to stop it.'

—Star Trek

'On the drive out here, you get yourself ready to enter the compartment of your life that is flying combat,' retired Col. Chris Chambliss told the *Los Angeles Times*.[169] 'And on the drive home, you get ready for that part of your life that's going to be the soccer game.'

And in between you kill.

Many people can relate to the banal experience of commuting to and from work and the constant struggle with trying to separate one's time in the office from time spent at home. But for an increasing number of Americans, the process of decompressing after a hard day's work is about more than just trying to forget about expense reports and the petty tyranny of office politics: in many cases, it's about trying to forget the lives you extinguished—and the lives of your comrades you couldn't save.

In contrast to the traditional notion of the war fighter on an actual battlefield, Col. Chambliss, who was based out of Nevada's Creech Air Force Base about forty minutes outside Las Vegas, could remotely order a Predator drone to fire a Hellfire missile at a group of suspected Taliban thousands of miles away in Afghanistan while, but a few hours later, making it home in time to catch a rerun of *Friends*. And there are thousands more just like him, soldiers and civilians alike, partaking in the US government's expanded use of UAVs to assassinate perceived enemies on the other side of the globe.

Creech is a tiny outpost in the barren Nevada desert, twenty miles north of a state prison and adjacent to a one-story casino. In a nondescript building, down a largely unmarked hallway, is a series of rooms, each with a rack of servers and a 'ground control station' for remotely controlling drones located 8,000 miles away. There, a drone pilot and a sensor operator sit in their flight suits in front of a series of screens.

In the pilot's hand is the joystick, guiding the drone as it soars above Afghanistan, Iraq, or some other battlefield. The sensor operator controls the cameras that bring the battlefield into full view to gain intelligence and hunt down targets. This team doesn't launch or land the plane—that is done by a similar team on the ground, closer to the battlefield. But once up in the air, the crew back in the US takes control.

Most US military drones are operated from Creech and another site just seven miles northeast of Las Vegas, Nellis Air Force Base. But weaponized drones have been remotely operated and/or monitored from dozens of military bases across the United States, including in Arizona, California, Florida, Indiana, Maryland, Missouri, New Mexico, New York, Ohio, North and South Dakota, and Texas.[170] Even the US Air Force Base in the Pacific island territory of Guam has become a staging ground for drone flights over Asia.

At Langley Air Force Base in Virginia, soldiers monitor live feeds from drones flying over Afghanistan—what they call 'Death TV.'[171] The *New York Times* reported that on a daily basis, the soldiers 'review 1,000 hours of video, 1,000 high-altitude spy photos and hundreds of hours of 'signals intelligence'—usually cellphone calls.' For up to twelve hours a day, they stare at ten overhead television screens, monitoring a constant stream of images being relayed to them from the battlefield while communicating on headsets with drone pilots at other bases and instant messaging with commanders on the ground. 'I'll have a phone in one ear, talking to a pilot on the headset in the other ear, typing in chat at the same time and watching screens,' a twenty-five-year-old first lieutenant told the *New York Times*. 'It's intense.'[172]

At the nearby CIA headquarters, meanwhile, civilians working for the spy agency work closely with agents in the field, as well as private military contractors, everywhere from Somalia to Pakistan to target both high-profile terror suspects, such as US citizen Anwar al-Awlaki, as well as those who merely fit the 'pattern of life' profile of a militant.[173]

Along with the new breed of killing technology has also come a new breed of pilot, one schooled in the 21st century ways of gaming and multi-tasking. Former UN Rapporteur Philip Alston has warned that with drone operators based so far away from the battlefield and undertaking operations entirely through computer screens and remote audio-feed, 'there is a risk of developing a "Playstation" mentality to killing'—but that's pretty much how this technology is designed.[174]

Those deeply involved in the military's UAV programs themselves say appealing to youth gaming culture was one of their explicit goals.[175] 'We modeled the controller after the PlayStation because that's what these eighteen-, nineteen-year-old Marines have been playing with all of their lives,' a robotics expert working for the Marines told author P.W. Singer in his book *Wired for War*.[176]

This can blur the line between the virtual and the real worlds. As a drone pilot in Qatar said, 'It's like a video game. It can get a little bloodthirsty. But it's fucking cool.'[177]

Not only have the controls on the military's war-fighting machines changed, so has the nature of armed conflict—not for those on the receiving end of Hellfire missiles, of course, but for those pulling the trigger. As Singer noted, 'For a new generation, "going to war" doesn't mean shipping off to some god-forsaken place to fight in a muddy foxhole but a daily commute in your Toyota Camry to sit behind a computer screen and drag a mouse.'

In addition to distancing soldiers from the consequences of their actions, the advent of remotely controlled drone warfare has changed the way the military trains its next generation of pilots, provoking what technology reporter Noah Schactman says is a 'military culture clash between teenaged videogamers and veteran flight jocks for control of the drones.' Drone pilots, after all, don't face any risk of dying in combat; thus, the disparaging label of 'cubicle warriors' applied to them by those who do.

'There is no valor in flying a remotely piloted aircraft,' Col. Luther Turner, a former fighter pilot turned drone operator, conceded to the *Washington Post*.[178]

But the future lies with the videogamers.

In 2004, the Air Force flew just five round-the-clock patrols with Predator and Reaper drones each day; by 2010, that number had reached forty.[179] By 2011, the Air Force was training more remote pilots than fighter and bomber pilots combined. There were about 1,100 drone pilots and 750 sensor operators in the Air Force by the end of 2011.[180] The Air Force projected that it would need at least 2,110 pilots and about 1,500 sensor operators to staff its fleet by 2015.

'Our #1 manning problem in the Air Force is manning our unmanned platform,' Dr. Mark T. Maybury, Chief Scientist at the Air Force, declared in a September 27, 2011 presentation.[181]

In order to meet that need, the Pentagon has hired an army of private contract employees.[182] At least a dozen defense contractors supply personnel to help the Air Force, special operations units, and the CIA. They work as technicians and mechanics, intelligence analysts and drone operators, sometimes even in the so-called kill chain when missiles are launched. This puts private contractors—people whose primary allegiance is to a corporation and who are not subject to the Uniform Code of Military Justice—smack in the middle of some of America's most sensitive military and intelligence operations.

The other measure the Pentagon has taken to meeting growing demand is to lower entry and training standards for those joining the military to operate drones. Air Force recruits, for example, do not have to meet the vision, physical or height requirements usually sought in a traditional pilot, nor do they have to go through the grueling courses for traditional pilots.

In 2009, the Air Force established two test programs at air bases in Nevada to train soldiers in the ways of drone warfare, one of them specifically geared to those who had never even flown a plane.[183] While traditional pilots usually train for two years before being deployed, this is a nine-month crash course, with six months dedicated to learning the basics of flying and the last few months to maneuvering a drone through a video-reproduction flight simulator.

In another program, drone pilots get 44 hours of cockpit training before they are sent to a squadron to be certified and allowed to command missions.[184] That compares with a minimum of 200 hours' training for pilots flying traditional warplanes. The Air Force decided to go with the fast-track training, where recruits spend forty hours in a basic Cessna-type plane before starting their drone training.

Cutting short the training required before a young soldier can pilot a killing machine in a combat zone has been controversial. 'We are creating the equivalent of a puppy mill,' one fighter pilot told the *Washington Post* in 2010. According to *Time* magazine, former General Mike Moseley, like other heads of the Air Force before him, is also a critic of letting non-pilots operate drones in potentially deadly battlefield situations, believing 'only a trained pilot [has] the mental and moral heft to deliver bombs and missiles.'[185]

It's not just a question of whether drone pilots possess the proper training to effectively employ lethal force abroad, though. It's also whether they can deal with the consequences of their actions. While those who operate drones are often located far from the battlefield, the high-resolution cameras on UAVs allow them to see, sometimes in gruesome detail, what happens when they decide to pull the trigger.

Fighter pilots 'come in at 500–600 mph, drop a 500-pound bomb and then fly away. You don't see what happens,' Col. Albert K. Aimar, commander of the 163rd Reconnaissance Wing based in southern California, explained to the Associated Press.[186] While the pilots who dropped atomic bombs on Hiroshima and Nagasaki killed hundreds of thousands of civilians, they did not see the effects firsthand. By contrast, those who pilot

Predator and Reaper drones see almost everything when they fire a missile. '[Y]ou watch it all the way to impact, and I mean it's very vivid, it's right there and personal,' said Aimar. 'So it does stay in people's minds for a long time.'

On the Al Jazeera show *The Stream,* former CentCom spokesman Josh Rushing described how an act so seemingly impersonal as remote-control killing can be just the opposite.[187] He said that sometimes drone pilots watch individuals and their families for days at a time, seeing them walk the dog and do their family chores. 'Man has never experienced this before—watching someone from above for so long without them knowing it, almost in a God-like way,' said Rushing. 'Then one day the decision comes down that you've got to take them out. You hit the button and kill them. But you knew these people in a way, so it can become quite personal.'

In his book *The Predator,* drone pilot Matt Martin expressed his anguish when he ended up killing civilians. In one case he described how he had carefully planned to blow up a group of supposed rebels who were standing around a truck. Suddenly, two kids on a bicycle appeared on the screen. There was an older boy, about ten, and a younger one balanced on the handlebars. They were laughing, talking—and riding alongside the truck.

Panicking, Martin wanted to stop the missile, but it was too late. The sensor operator had already released it. 'Mesmerized by approaching calamity, we could only stare in abject horror as the silent missile bore down upon them out of the sky.... When the screens cleared, I saw the bicycle blown twenty feet away. One of the tires was still spinning. The bodies of the two little boys lay bent and broken among the bodies of the insurgents.'[188]

Martin soothed his conscience by recalling the words of Secretary of Defense Robert McNamara that 'you must sometimes do evil in order to do good.' (This is the same McNamara who bears much of the responsibility for the Vietnamese War [known in Vietnam as 'the American War'] that killed over two million Vietnamese and some fifty thousand US soldiers.)

US Major Bryan Callahan said that drone pilots are taught 'early and often' to compartmentalize their lives, to separate the time they spend firing missiles on battlefields from the time they spend—the same day—at home with their families.[189] When it comes to witnessing murder, 'you need to tuck those things away and put them where they belong,' Callahan explains. 'We're pretty good at it.'

They'd better be. Because despite drones possessing the latest in imaging technology and despite all the much-vaunted checks that go into the decision to deploy lethal force, mistakes are all too common. And it's hard to go home to one's own family after wiping out someone else's.

The *Los Angeles Times* detailed a lengthy investigation into a tragic incident in Afghanistan that left roughly two dozen civilians dead.[190] In the early morning hours of February 21, 2010, US Air Force pilots thought they had found the jackpot: a convoy of Taliban militants closing in on a group of American soldiers just a few miles away—a perfect, textbook case of the surveillance and precision power of drones in action. Every 'i' was dotted, every 't' was crossed.

'We have eighteen pax [passengers] dismounted and spreading out at this time,' said a Predator drone pilot at Creech Air Force Base in Nevada, one of US military's most experienced who had spent more than one thousand hours training others to fly UAVs.

'They're praying. They are praying,' said the drone's camera operator. 'This is definitely it, this is their force,' said the cameraman. 'Praying? I mean, seriously, that's what they do.'

'They're gonna do something nefarious,' added the drone crew's intelligence coordinator.

While they were sure they had a 'sweet target,' in the words of the cameraman, the Americans did not fire. They still had more checks and balances to go through.

In addition to the pilot, cameraman and intelligence officer stationed at Creech Air Force Base, there was also a team of screeners at Eglin Air Force Base in Okaloosa, Florida, tasked with carefully monitoring the Predator's video feeds and sending their observations to those piloting the drone. Meanwhile, an Army captain on the ground in Afghanistan leading US troops near the suspected Taliban had the final word on whether to fire.

Though the crew had their suspicions about the convoy, they could not fire until they had what they believed to be definitive proof they were dealing with armed insurgents. At one point, the Predator pilot in Nevada thought he spotted a weapon. But the camera operator could not confirm it. 'I was hoping we could make a rifle out,' the pilot complained. 'Never mind.'

Then a screener in Florida reported possibly seeing one or more children in the suspected Taliban convoy. 'Bull[—]. Where!?' the camera operator replied. 'I don't think they have kids out at this hour.'

'Why didn't he say "possible" child?' the pilot said. 'Why are they so quick to call kids but not to call a rifle?'

'I really doubt that children call,' the cameraman responded. 'Man, I really... hate that,' he added, before qualifying: 'Well, maybe a teenager.'

The pilot told the troops on the ground of the screeners' observations, saying they had spotted 'a possible rifle and two possible children near the SUV.' As if it was a game of telephone, the original message about identifying children had become 'possible children.' And the 'possible rifle' became proof positive that the convoy possessed weapons. Ultimately, the Army captain decided it was time to fire, pointing to a 'positive identification' he had made based on 'the weapons we've identified and the demographics of the individuals'—demographics, not identities—as well as intercepted phone conversations picked up from somewhere in the region.

The consequences were grave. 'Dead and wounded were everywhere,' the *Times* reports. In the aftermath of the strike, the Predator crew noticed three survivors trying to surrender.

'What are those?' said the cameraman.

'Women and children,' the intelligence coordinator replied.

'That lady is carrying a kid, huh?' said the pilot.

'The baby, I think, on the right. Yeah,' the intelligence coordinator said.

Having just massacred a group of civilians, the crew tried to tell themselves that they did nothing wrong—that they were just doing their jobs.

'No way to tell, man,' the safety observer said.

'No way to tell from here,' said the cameraman.

For all the military's vaunted checks and balances, for all of its screeners and intelligence coordinators and safety observers, the Predator drone crew had just killed innocent men, women, and children. According to the US government, fifteen people were killed and twelve wounded, including three kids. According to Afghans, twenty-three people were killed, including two young children aged three and four.

For many soldiers, the forty-minute commute home is not enough time to decompress and forget horrors like that—even when the ones they've killed are militants, not civilians. As Col. Chris Chambliss put it: 'To go to work, and to do bad things to bad people, and then when I go home and go to church and try to be a productive member of society, those don't necessarily mesh well.'

When pilots go home, they don't talk about the bad people—or innocent civilians—they've killed. Instead, they bottle it up inside. A pilot identified only as 'Captain Dan' told producers for a documentary on drones that his family knows he flies UAVs, but 'I don't go home and tell them what mission I flew or something like that. That's a challenge in the job that you have to do day in and day out.'[191]

Col. Scott Brenton, a drone pilot operating out of Hancock Field Air Base in upstate New York, acknowledged the disconnect of fighting a telewar from his padded seat in suburbia. 'It's a strange feeling,' he said, describing how he steps out of a dark room full of video screens, his adrenaline still surging after squeezing the trigger, and rushes home to help with homework. 'No one in my immediate environment is aware of anything that occurred.'[192]

While drone pilots may quietly suffer from combat-related stress, many soldiers relish the idea of engaging in combat missions while remaining at home, pointing to the burden and worry it takes off their families and the opportunity it provides them to spend more time with their kids.[193] The family of a drone pilot doesn't have to deal with the stress of wondering if their loved one will make it back alive.

Drone pilots sit safely, thousands of miles away from the physical danger of the war they are fighting. The only danger they face is mental. But that is still a very real danger—one that, in extreme cases, can boil out into home life in the form of abuse and the break up of families.

For drone pilots and other drone crew members, viewing the real-time video feed is often the biggest stressor related to post-traumatic stress disorder (PTSD). Soldiers on the ground engage in brutal and deadly combat—and drone operators watch. That exacts a toll.

A December 2011 government-commissioned report of Air Force drone pilots found that nearly half reported 'high operational stress,' in contrast to 36 percent of a control group of 600 Air Force members in logistics or support jobs.[194] Nearly a third of the US Air Force's 1,100 drone operators suffered 'burnout,' with 17 percent thought to be 'clinically distressed,' though much of that distress may have come as the result of earlier deployments.

Pilots operating drones that are supporting US troops in war zones like Afghanistan have an easier time because they have a sense of accomplishment from protecting troops on the ground. An Air Force major from the base at Creech recalled how grateful the US ground troops in Afghanistan were when he flew a Reaper above them for five hours one night so they could get some sleep—without anyone sneaking up on them.[195]

Soldiers and Marines who get pinned down in insurgent fire in Afghanistan often call in the drones for help, and directly communicate with drone operators to get precise targets. 'These guys are up above firing at the enemy,' said Colonel McDonald, co-author of the study.[196] 'They love that, they feel like they're protecting our people. They build this virtual relationship with the guys on the ground.'

'Physically, we may be in Vegas,' Air Force Major Shannon Rogers told *Time* magazine in 2005, 'but mentally, we are flying over Iraq. It feels real.'[197]

'A lot of people downplay it, saying "You're eight thousand miles away. What's the big deal?" But it's not really eight thousand miles away, it's eighteen inches away,' Col. Pete Gersten, commander of the 432nd Air Expeditionary Wing at Creech, told *Stars and Stripes* in 2009.[198] 'We're closer in a majority of ways than we've ever been as a service.'

'I've seen troops die before,' sensor operator Jesse Grace told the military paper. In one incident, Grace watched as an IED killed five of his comrades. All he could do was watch. 'I felt like I was helpless,' Grace said. 'It was a traumatic experience. It shocked me. I had just turned nineteen. It happened on Memorial Day. I remember that.' Many drone pilots have witnessed similar events and are just as affected by 'survivor's guilt' as if they were like any other soldier who was party to a firefight.

'If I screw up or miss something, if I screw up a shot, I wish it was me down there, not them. Sometimes I feel like I left them behind,' said US Major Bryan Callahan.[199]

The Air Force study found that the biggest source of stress for drone operators was long hours and frequent shift changes because of staff shortages. Drone crews work ten- to twelve-hour shifts. Alternating between day, evening and overnight shifts every three weeks prevents them from fully integrating into civilian life.[200]

As a result, drone crews are generally 'tired, disgruntled and disillusioned,' said a former fighter pilot who teaches at the Air Force Academy. 'It's insane,' he said. 'You can't run an Air Force like this without burning your people out.'

Many pilots complain of sheer boredom. 'For most missions, nothing happens. Your plane orbits in the sky, you watch and you wait. It's very boring. I'd much rather be flying an F-16,' said fighter-pilot-turned-MIT-professor Missy Cummings.[201]

Drone pilot Matt Martin recalled how, after months and months of long days staring at monitors, he became bored, cynical and suspicious of everyone he was watching. And, as the military are wont to do, he found himself hoping that the targets he was following would prove themselves to be insurgents so he could 'get some action.'

One day, he spotted a group of men at a park in Iraq's Sadr City, and wondered if it was a terrorist cell meeting or just a bunch of men smoking and dancing. He watched them for hours.

'One of the men eventually got up off the ground and walked over to a nearby shack. I thought I finally had them. He was going for weapons,' Martin wrote. Alas, the man returned with folding chairs. Martin was disappointed. 'I kept hoping somebody would pull out a rocket launcher,' he admitted. 'At least it would mean I was making good use of the Predator's time and resources. Beside, blowing up things was much more interesting than watching men sit around in the dark smoking cigarettes, dancing and holding hands.'[202]

Another major problem drone personnel deal with is information overload. Tasked with sifting through unprecedented amounts of raw data to help the military determine what targets to hit and what to avoid, drone-based sensors find themselves drowning in a sea of endless data. And they are not alone. 'There is information overload at every level of the military—from the general to the soldier on the ground,' said neuroscientist Art Kramer, a researcher contracted by the military to help soldiers cope with digital overload that has led not only to stress, but to tragic mistakes.[203]

The military seems to be aware of the insanity. 'It's clear that we've pushed our units not to the breaking point, but close,' said Col. Eric Mathewson, commander of the Air Force's Unmanned Aerial Systems Task Force. But it doesn't seem the military is doing much about it.

An interview request issued to the Veterans Affairs National Center for Post Traumatic Stress Disorder (NCPTSD) for this book was denied, with a spokesperson declaring that NCPTSD 'does not have a subject matter expert to deal with your request.' Even though there are numerous interviews and books written on the topic of drone pilots experiencing symptoms related to PTSD, there is no official governmental expert who can speak about it.

It seems that the military has another solution in mind—replace the pilots with automated, autonomous killing machines.[204]

Already, the human role in drone warfare is rapidly becoming that of 'a supervisor who serves in a fail-safe capacity in the event of a system malfunction,' notes retired Army Colonel Thomas Adams.[205] Even then, Adams thinks that the speed, confusion, and information overload of modern-day war will soon move the whole process outside 'human space.' Future weapons 'will be too fast, too small, too numerous, and will create an environment too complex for humans to direct,' he says, and new technologies 'are rapidly taking us to a place where we may not want to go, but probably are unable to avoid.'

The trend toward greater autonomy will only increase as the military moves from one pilot remotely flying one drone to one pilot remotely managing several drones at once. 'Lethal autonomy is inevitable,' said Ronald C.

Arkin, who authored a study on the subject for the Army Research Office.[206]

Arkin believes autonomous drones could be programmed to abide by international law. Others vehemently disagree and question the ethics of robots making life and death decisions.

But one thing is certain: autonomous weapons won't suffer from PTSD. And that's why—ethical or not—the military will most likely be expanding its dependency on machines that do not possess the troublesome emotions and consciences of its human pilots.

5

Remote-controlled Victims

'The Khan family never heard it. They had been sleeping for an hour when a Hellfire missile pierced their mud hut. Black smoke and dust choked the villagers as they dug through the rubble. Four-year-old Zeerak's legs were severed. His sister Maria, three, was badly scorched. Both were dead. When their cousin Irfan, 16, saw them, he gently curled them into his arms, squeezed the rumpled bodies to his chest, lightly kissed their faces, and slid into a stupor.'

—Los Angeles Times[207]

'Never before in the history of warfare have we been able to distinguish as well between combatants and civilians as we can with drones.'

—Wall Street Journal editorial[208]

Eking out a living among the stark, barren landscape of a remote land, known little even to their own country-folk and utterly anonymous to those in faraway America, more hapless victims could hardly be found than the people of the Federally Administered Tribal Areas in northwest Pakistan. It was only in the decade after 9/11 that their anonymity became a fatal burden, counted in an ever-increasing number of lost lives.

Beginning in 2004, when the CIA expanded its search for militants from the Afghan border into Pakistan, the regions of North and South Waziristan began to be pelted by missiles fired from UAVs.

Before they fired, they hovered—their onerous, ominous buzzing casting shadows over village schools and homes, over weddings and funerals. The villagers never knew when they would fire, whether it would be at dawn, before the household woke for morning prayers, or when the men had left for the mosque, or in the middle of the day when bread baked in ovens and children played in courtyards.

The attacks in Pakistan, carried out via the CIA's covert program, began in June 2004 with a strike against Pakistani Taliban commander Nek Muhammad that killed six to eight people, including two children—a fact rarely reported. The Pakistani military initially took credit for the attack and denied US involvement, but it later became clear that this was the first US drone strike in Pakistan.[209]

As the years wore on, the number of drone strikes grew and grew and grew, especially under President Obama. When George Bush was president, the US carried out forty-five to fifty-two drone strikes in Pakistan; President Obama carried out six times that number in his first term alone. On October 14, 2011, the grisly remote-controlled war reached a new milestone when the three-hundredth drone strike took place in the early hours of dawn, killing six alleged militants.[210]

The Hellfire missiles that come hurling down from the sky can instantly incinerate their victims, or kill them with flying shrapnel or powerful blast waves capable of crushing internal organs. Survivors often suffer painful wounds and disfiguring burns, limb amputations, vision loss, and hearing loss. With poor government services and extreme poverty, survivors can face a lifetime of misery and pain.

US authorities do not provide compensation to civilian strike victims in Pakistan, although they do in Afghanistan. In some cases, Pakistani authorities have offered limited compensation, but these offers are not only inadequate to address the damage but are also usually rejected by the victims on principle.

Since the areas where the drones strike have been sealed off by the Pakistani security forces, journalists have not been able to enter the area and report on the damage in lives, property, and livelihoods that is being inflicted on Pakistan's drone-battered northwest. Some reports rely on local untrained journalists working with news agencies and other civilian sources, but locals are often reluctant to speak for fear of retaliation from all sides in the conflict—the Taliban, the Pakistani military and US operatives in their midst. Other reports rely on Pakistani and US intelligence agencies, which tend to label every kill a militant.

The number of strikes themselves may be underreported, given the initial effort by the Pakistani government to pretend the strikes were Pakistani helicopter strikes or accidental explosions, and given that the strikes often take place in very remote areas.

Reporting on women and children is particularly problematic. In the traditional, conservative culture of Waziristan, families live in large compounds surrounded by high walls; the women and children live separately from the men. Male neighbors often don't even know how many women and children live in another family's compound. Reporters are not allowed to talk to, much less photograph, women.

Then there is the issue of who is a civilian and who is a militant. With the Obama administration defining every military-age male in the strike zone as a combatant, it's easy to see why there are such widely varying statistics about the number of casualties, especially regarding civilians.

These stats for civilians killed start at zero, the intellectually insulting figure given in June 2011 by John O. Brennan, President Obama's top counterterrorism adviser. He said, speaking about the preceding year, 'there hasn't been a single collateral death because of the exceptional proficiency, precision of the capabilities we've been able to develop.'[211] Mr. Brennan later adjusted his statement somewhat, saying, 'Fortunately, for more than a year, due to our discretion and precision, the US government has not found credible evidence of collateral deaths resulting from US counterterrorism operations outside of Afghanistan or Iraq.'

According to statistics kept by the New America Foundation, from 2004–2011, between 1,717 and 2,680 individuals were killed, and of those, between 293 and 471 were civilians.[212] The UK-based Bureau of Investigative Journalism puts those figures higher, saying that between 2,372 and 2,997 were killed in that timeframe. Of those, between 391 and 780 were civilians, 175 of them children.[213]

The Bureau's figures are probably more accurate, as it is one of the few groups that actually does have sources on the ground. In fact, they help get the voices of the victims themselves out from the war-battered region to challenge official accounts of the drone war and the deception that drones are a foolproof method of killing militants without collateral damage.

Shahzad Akbar, a Pakistani lawyer who has been representing drone victims and who started the group Foundation for Fundamental Rights, disputes even these figures and claims that the vast majority of those killed are ordinary civilians. 'I have a problem with this word "militant." Most of the victims who are labeled militants might be Taliban sympathizers but they are not involved in any criminal or terrorist acts,' he claimed. He said the Americans often use the fact that someone carries a weapon as proof they're a combatant. 'If that's the criteria then the US will have to commit genocide, because all men in that area carry AK-47s and all believe in Sharia law. That is part of their culture. Since when can we kill people for their beliefs?' Shahzad believes that only those people whom the Americans label 'high-value targets' should be considered militants; all others should be considered civilian victims.

Noor Behram, a photographer who is constantly putting his life at risk to photograph the aftermath of drone strikes, agreed. 'For every ten to fifteen people killed, maybe they get one militant,' he said.[214]

The US government prefers to stick to the myth that drone strikes are only killing militants. According to the official story, the tribal areas of Pakistan are infested with militants, shadowy figures planning acts of mass murder in the region's stark caves and crannies that harbor the world's worst terrorists—and that these, the worst of the worst, are the only ones being killed.

And US officials have been getting away with telling that story, since corporate media outlets are more interested in running unverified government spin as 'news' than talking to people on the ground to actually uncover the truth. Like clockwork, after every drone strike purporting to kill a handful of militants, an anonymous US government official speaks to the press, calmly reassuring reporters that only bad people die in America's drone wars. And the press eats it up.

The American government also plays the press by highlighting the supposedly big-time militant ringleaders it executes without trial; victories that help assuage any concerns about civilian deaths among the faint-hearted.

On August 7, 2009, when the rest of the news from the War on Terror offered a decidedly bleak picture, a drone attack in the village of Zanghara in South Waziristan killed Baitullah Mehsud, the leader of the Tehreek-e-Taliban Pakistan and alleged mastermind of the assassination of Pakistan's former Prime Minister Benazir Bhutto.[215]

According to the report, Mehsud had been at the home of his father-in-law receiving an intravenous treatment for diabetes when a missile fired from a Predator drone rained down on the building and killed him. Scant mention was made of his wife, father-in-law and eight others who were killed as well. And there was no mention that this successful strike had been preceded by fifteen other unsuccessful strikes aimed at killing Mehsud—strikes that instead caused the death of between 204 and 321 victims, from low-level Taliban to elderly tribal leaders to children.[216] All the American public heard was that justice had been done now that the evil Mehsud was dead.

Two years and many less-touted drone strikes later, on June 3, 2011—a bare month after a helicopter raid by Navy Seals succeeded in killing Osama bin Laden at his compound in Abbotabad—another top Al Qaeda leader, Ilyas Kashmiri, was also mowed down by a US Predator drone.[217] Kashmiri, referred to as Pakistan's most dangerous militant, was considered responsible for several attacks on Pakistani security forces. These included an attack just one week earlier on a Pakistani naval base in Karachi in which two anti-submarine aircraft were destroyed.[218] Kashmiri was also alleged to be the mastermind for the terrorist attacks in Mumbai, India, in 2008, which killed 163 people. His death was greeted as a victory by both American and Pakistani forces, though the latter had also claimed him dead after a drone attack in 2009.

What actually happened in that 2009 attack is one of the many buried tragedies.[219] On September 7, 2009, throughout the day two drones were hovering over the skies of Mirali Tehsil in North Waziristan. It was the month of Ramadan and people in the area were angry that the drones were interfering in their religious activities. They were also scared, but in Pashtun culture showing one's fear is cowardice and a matter of shame, so the fear was left unspoken.

Fifteen-year-old Sadaullah, a local student, was particularly happy that day as there was an *iftar* (breaking of the fast) feast planned at his house that evening. His grandfather and uncles were coming, and his mother was cooking his favorite meal. Sadaullah saw the unmanned machine in the air and joked with his friends about the '*bangana*,' a local name given to drones in the area due to the constant noise they make.

In the evening, the house was crowded with all the men in the family—his grandfathers, uncles, and cousins. Everyone broke their fast and proceeded to the courtyard for prayers.

The lucky ones had already re-entered the house when the missile struck. Not Sadaullah. He fell unconscious under the debris of the fallen roof. When he awoke at a hospital in Peshawar, he was blind in one eye from the shrapnel and both his legs had been amputated. He later learned that his elderly uncle, who had been in a wheelchair, was dead, as were two of his cousins, Kadaanullah Jan and Sabir-ud-Din.

'I had a dream to be a doctor,' said Sadaullah, 'But now I can't even walk to school.' So he studies religion in the village madrasa and has little hope for the future.

Meanwhile, the media reported that the strike had been a success, killing a group of militants, including Ilyas Kashmiri. It was not until two years later that Kashmiri was actually killed.

The hubbub surrounding the drone killings of Taliban and Al Qaeda leaders like Baitullah Mehsud and Ilyas Kashmiri is notable because it illustrates the strategy and rhetoric that has gone into the elevation of drone warfare as the best possible solution to the strategic challenges posed by non-state actors hiding in remote outposts of the world. The intense focus on men like Mehsud and Kashmiri, who by any measure had a damnable lack of respect for human life, prevents any questioning of the tactics and their impact on less dastardly people—like innocent men, women, and children. 'Don't you want the bad guys to die?' is the question used to suppress those inconvenient, nagging doubts about drones and their hidden victims.

Unsurprisingly, there are many others dead than just these bad guys—the evil poster boys of Al Qaeda and the Taliban whose deaths made everything else seem justified and unworthy of debate. Slowly, despite the muzzled silence imposed on them by local security forces and the indifference of the media, the victims of drone attacks whose houses were felled, loved ones killed and solitude destroyed by the constant buzzing of invasive aircraft, began to speak.

One of them was Karim Khan, a resident of the tiny village of Machikhel, near Mir Ali in North Waziristan. On December 31, 2009, as most Americans were putting together their lists of New Year resolutions and gearing up for an evening of festivities to bid adieu to the first decade of the millennium, a drone strike leveled the *hujra*, or community space, located within the four walls of Karim Khan's compound.[220] Karim Khan's family had used the space for years to organize the community for *jirgas*, or gatherings in which community members made decisions regarding issues that affected their tiny village, from pooling money for the medical care of an elderly relative to mediating a property dispute between brothers.

But there was not a jirga in process that evening. Indeed, Khan was not even in the village that night—he was hundreds of miles away in Islamabad. His brother Asif Iqbal and his eighteen-year-old son Zaeenullah Khan were home, though. They were chatting in the courtyard when a drone flew overhead, casting its dark, buzzing shadow over the hearths of the village of Machikhel.

But that night it didn't just hover above, watching the movements of the villagers below, as it had done on other occasions. No, this time it let loose a missile into the very heart of the village. When the chaos of the explosion dissipated, and the ever-encroaching darkness settled back over the rubble and the blood, Khan's brother and son had been blown to bits.

Khan did not know of their deaths until it was almost morning, when a ringing cell phone at his bedside delivered the news. He rushed home to lift the biers of his beloved brother and son, burying their bodies—on New Years Day, 2010—in the dry cold soil of the village they had loved. News reports alleged that the target of the drone had been Haji Omar, a Taliban commander. But the villagers insisted that Haji Omar had been nowhere near the village that night. The tragedy that forever scarred the lives of Karim Khan's family was the product of a mistake.

While the American public hears stories about evil militants like Ilyas Kashmiri and Baitullah Mehsud, it doesn't hear the stories about victims like Asif Iqbal and Zaeenullah Khan.

Indeed, Asif Iqbal was not a militant or even a militant sympathizer, but a schoolteacher. After receiving his masters in English literature from the National University of Modern Languages, he had returned to work as a schoolteacher in the adjoining village of Dattakhel. It was a post he had held for eight years, teaching children with whatever meager resources he could muster. For nearly a decade he had weathered threats and school closures enforced by the Taliban, and smiled through the restrictions placed by Pakistani security forces. Iqbal bravely confronted the myriad challenges of educating a population riven by war, arguing for the distant benefits of education against the instant power of firearms.

This educated man who had put his faith in the promise of the future was now dead, the target of a faraway aggressor he would never know, an aggressor who would face no punishment for pressing the 'fire' button without looking long enough, without checking and double-checking the target. Iqbal left behind a young family. His bride of three years was now a widow so distraught that she could not speak for weeks after the attack. In her lap was Mohammad Kafeel, a two-year-old boy who would never remember his father, save for the worn, fingered photographs shown to him by his mother, a single newspaper clipping describing the attack, and the memories told to him by old uncles and cousins.

Also murdered that night was Karim Khan's son, Zaeenullah Khan, a recent graduate from high school. The boy had returned to the village inspired by his young uncle and got a job as a guard in the same modest school. Like his uncle, he was determined to convince the community of the value of education. He died close to his mentor that night, leaving behind hundreds of students with scant chance of resuming their education—young people now mired in hatred for the drone that had killed their teacher, aching for revenge.

A third man died that night, too, a chance visitor to the hujra in Karim Khan's compound. He was a stonemason who had traveled to the little town to work on the village mosque. Too tired after the day's labor to return to his own home miles away, he had been welcomed—with the traditional hospitality—as a guest in Khan's home.

The casualties from the attack on Machikhel village that night would have slipped into the same murky abyss as hundreds of nameless, faceless casualties of drone attacks, labeled with the sterile inhumanity of 'collateral damage,' but for the fact that Karim Khan was a journalist.

After burying the bodies of his son and brother that grim, gray January, he vowed that they would never be forgotten. Over the next year, he gathered victims' families from all over North and South Waziristan, the detritus of drones pushed out of the world's moral narrative, their suffering unseen, and their plight invisible before the gigantic imperative of killing terrorists.

In November 2010, Khan won his first small victory. With the help of an Islamabad-based human rights lawyer named Shahzad Akbar, he sent a legal notice to the American embassy in Islamabad, detailing the wrongful deaths of his brother and son, and accusing the CIA of grossly violating the Universal Declaration of Human Rights in its targeting and killing of innocent civilians through drone attacks.[221]

A few weeks later, close to the first anniversary of the attack, Karim Khan spoke outside a police station where he had just lodged a complaint, asking that the CIA Station Chief in Islamabad be forbidden from leaving Pakistan until he answered to the charges against him. 'We appeal to the authorities to not let Jonathan Banks escape from Pakistan,' Khan implored, standing on the station steps.[222] His lawyer, Shahzad Akbar, said that his client had learned of Mr. Banks's identity, normally kept secret, through local press reports. A local Pakistani newspaper had also reported that the Station Chief's name was not on the roster of diplomats slated to receive diplomatic immunity, and claimed that he should be made to answer for the atrocities inflicted by the CIA drone program on innocent Pakistani civilians.[223]

While the accusation by the family of drone victims against a CIA agent made headlines in Pakistan, Karim Khan did not win that round. Jonathan Banks, if that was even his real name, was allowed to leave the country. But in the ensuing days and months, Khan's work organizing the families of victims slowly began to bear fruit as local politicians in Pakistan and international human rights organizations like the UK-based legal services group Reprieve and the international rights organization CIVIC began to look more deeply into the issue.

One of the worst drone attacks occurred on March 17, 2011, when a community in North Waziristan was holding a community meeting, a jirga, to settle a dispute about a nearby chromite mine. All the local leaders attended, including thirty-five government-appointed tribal leaders. From the CIA perspective, this must have looked like a Taliban gathering, for they sent in the drones, killing forty-two of the most respected members of the community.

In October 2011, the Pakistan-based Foundation for Fundamental Rights, with the help of the British legal group Reprieve, brought a group of elders and drone victim families from North and South Waziristan to Islamabad. Called the 'Grand Waziristan Jirga,' it gathered over 350 villagers, including over sixty drone victim families who lived on the Pakistani-Afghan frontier to meet with Westerners. For the first time, the villagers got a chance to offer their perspectives on the shadowy drone war being waged in their region. The jirga ended with a call from the Pakistanis condemning all forms of terrorism, including the CIA-operated drone strikes.

In the group was a shy sixteen-year-old boy named Tariq Aziz. Tariq had been trained by human rights lawyer Shahzad Akbar in basic photography so that he could document the devastation caused by the strikes in his own and adjoining villages.[224] Tariq had a personal motivation: eighteen months earlier, his cousin Anwar Ullah had been killed by an unmanned drone as he drove his motorcycle through the village of Norak.

Tariq also had plenty of firsthand experience with drones. Neil Williams, a British investigator with Reprieve who was at the tribal meeting, recalled having asked Tariq if he had ever seen a drone. 'I expected him to say, "Yes, I see one a week." But he said they saw ten or fifteen every day,' said Williams. 'And he was saying at nighttime, it was making him crazy, because he couldn't sleep.'

When the meeting ended, Tariq returned to his village in Waziristan, encouraged in his documenting efforts by the activists and journalists who vowed to publicize the plight of Waziris. But neither he nor the foreigners he met with could have imagined that the first documentation of drone deaths after their gathering in Islamabad would be that of Tariq himself.

Three days after the meeting, Tariq, together with his twelve-year-old cousin Waheed Rehman, went to pick up his newlywed aunt. When the two boys were just two hundred yards from her house, two missiles slammed into their car, killing them both instantly.

According to the Bureau of Investigative Journalism, their deaths marked the 174th and 175th child casualties of CIA drones.[225]

Tariq Aziz was the youngest of seven children, growing up dirt poor along the hardscrabble border between Afghanistan and Pakistan. His father had left years ago, working as a driver for a sheikh in the United Arab Emirates and sending money home to his family whenever he could. His cousin Waheed was equally poor, his family relying on the boy's monthly salary of $23 as a shop assistant to make stretched ends meet.

Thanks to the fateful meeting in Islamabad days before, the death of these boys—unlike other drone victims never mentioned or mourned beyond the village—was reported in newspapers around the world. American lawyer Clive Stafford Smith, who had just met the boy in Islamabad, wrote a compelling *New York Times* Op-Ed.[226] 'My mistake had been to see the drone war in Waziristan in terms of abstract legal theory—as a blatantly illegal invasion of Pakistan's sovereignty, akin to President Richard M. Nixon's bombing of Cambodia in 1970,' Stafford wrote. 'But now, the issue has suddenly become very real and personal. Tariq was a good kid, and courageous. My warm hand recently touched his in friendship; yet, within three days, his would be cold in death, the rigor mortis inflicted by my government. And Tariq's extended family, so recently hoping to be our allies for peace, has now been ripped apart by an American missile—most likely making any effort we make at reconciliation futile.'

A US official acknowledged to ABC News that the

attack was not a mistake—the CIA had chosen this target because the two people in the car were supposedly militants.[227] Pratap Chatterje, a journalist at the Bureau of Investigative Journalism who met Tariq at the Islamabad meeting, was dumbfounded. 'If this sixteen-year-old was indeed a suspected terrorist, then why wasn't he arrested in Islamabad?' Chatterje asked. 'It would have been very easy to find him at the hotel and arrest him.'[228]

On November 4, 2011, two days after the attack that killed the boys, the *Wall Street Journal* reported on a dispute within the Obama administration regarding drone attacks, saying that many key US military and State Department officials were demanding that the strikes be more selective while CIA brass wanted a free hand to pursue suspected militants. The dispute led to an independent review of the program during the summer of 2011—a review in which President Obama himself was involved. According to the *Journal*, the CIA agreed to make a series of 'secret concessions,' including giving the State Department greater say in strike decisions; informing Pakistani leaders in advance about more operations; and suspending operations when Pakistani officials visited the US.[229]

Too bad there were no Pakistani officials visiting the US when Tariq Aziz and Waheed Khan were driving to their aunt's house.

The consequences of drones go beyond the deaths, injuries, and property damage, and the emotional trauma that injured victims and surviving family members face. A key study by Stanford and NYU Law Schools released in October 2012 called 'Living Under Drones'[230] exposed an often overlooked but critical aspect: how the constant hovering of drones and the uncertainty about if and when they might strike terrorizes men, women and children and has a profound impact on community life.[231] This was something I also found when I talked to residents of Waziristan during my 2012 visit to Pakistan.

There are some 800,000 people living in Waziristan, and many of them live in a state of constant fear. Whether they are working on their farms, performing their chores, going to the market, driving their cars, or just sitting at home, they are always worried a drone might strike. Their inability to protect themselves and their loved ones compounds the stress. So does their inability to hold anyone accountable.

Safdar Dawar, president of the Tribal Union of Journalists, the main association of journalists in the areas affected by US drones, told Stanford researchers, 'If I am walking in the market, I have this fear that maybe the person walking next to me is going to be a target of the drone. If I'm shopping, I'm really careful and scared. If I'm standing on the road and there is a car parked next to me, I never know if that is going to be the target. Maybe they will target the car in front of me or behind me. Even in mosques, if we're praying, we're worried that maybe one person who is standing with us praying is wanted. So, wherever we are, we have this fear of drones.'[232]

A humanitarian worker who had worked in Waziristan

said: 'Do you remember 9/11? Do you remember what it felt like right after? I was in New York on 9/11. I remember people crying in the streets. People were afraid about what might happen next. People didn't know if there would be another attack. There was tension in the air. This is what it is like. It is a continuous tension, a feeling of continuous uneasiness. We are scared. You wake up with a start to every noise.'

Residents I met with said they had a hard time sleeping, that many people suffer from depression and PTSD, and that there is a widespread use of anti-depressants and anti-anxiety medications. They also reported a spate of suicides, something they said never existed before.

Some families are afraid to send their children to school, some children beg not to be sent to school, and teachers are often afraid to work in the drone-strike areas. 'These fears are not without a legitimate basis, as drones have reportedly struck schools in the past, resulting in extensive damage to educational infrastructure, as well as the deaths of dozens of children,' the 'Living Under Drones' study reported.

The people said their fear of drones keeps them away from social gatherings and makes it difficult to carry out day-to-day activities and hold community functions. A Waziri told me, 'We don't want to socialize anymore; we're afraid to get together like we used to do. People stay in their own homes now.'

Even the solemn rituals related to death and funerals have been altered. Since drone victims are often incinerated, with body parts—if indeed there are any—left in pieces and unidentifiable, traditional burial processes are impossible. And with drone strikes having targeted funerals and spaces where families have gathered to offer condolences to the deceased, families are unable to hold their traditional dignified burials.

One of the most troubling consequences is the erosion of the jirga system, the community-based conflict resolution process that is fundamental to Pashtun society. If unable to hold meetings, members of the community have no way to resolve conflicts.

Also undermining community values is the horrendous US practice of striking one area multiple times ('double taps'). With rescuers having been killed for their humanitarian efforts to help the wounded, both community members and humanitarian workers are often afraid to assist the injured.

US drone strikes have sown fear, as well as mistrust. Many Waziris believe that paid informants help the CIA identify potential targets, including placing small tracking devices, often referred to as 'chips,' in vehicles or houses.

Whether true or not, these beliefs have bred an intense fear of outsiders, as well as widespread division within the community. Neighbors suspect neighbors of spying for US, Pakistani, or Taliban intelligence.

The Taliban and Al Qaeda are fierce in dealing with people they consider snitches. There are death squads associated with Al Qaeda and the Taliban—called Khorasan Mujahedin—that show up after drone attacks to hunt down informants they suspect of helping the Americans identify targets.[233] Informants, often poor villagers, are paid about $100 for information about militants and their safe houses.

Seeking revenge, forty to sixty heavily armed and hooded men descend on a village, kidnapping their victims. Most of those kidnapped are beaten, tortured and killed, with videotapes of their executions passed around as a warning to others. 'Interestingly, there is a parallel between the Khorasan and Americans,' said Shahzad Akbar. 'Both use torture to extract information from their detainees, who say anything to be spared from the torture. And in the end, both get their bad guys.'

'In the sky there are drones, and on the ground there's Khorasan Mujahedin,' one of the villagers told the *Los Angeles Times*.[234] 'Villagers are extremely terrorized. Whenever there's a drone strike, within 24 hours Khorasan Mujahedin comes in and takes people away.' The drone attacks stoke an endless fire of violence and revenge.

Then there are the hundreds of thousands of indirect victims—villagers caught between CIA-operated drones, the pernicious politics of the Pakistani Taliban and operations by the Pakistani military to 'cleanse' the area of alleged militants. This volatile mix has led to the destruction of village after village, and the plight of local villagers seems to be of little concern to any of the parties involved.

Even when the Pakistani military declared many areas safe for families to return, the absence of reconstruction assistance and the persistence of drone attacks in the region have kept many from doing so.

The flight of so many refugees has affected an even

greater population—the people of the southern port city of Karachi. There are no visible drones flying over this mega-city of nearly 18 million people, but its squalid, bursting streets have had to absorb massive numbers of families fleeing the conflict in the Northwest.[235] A report produced by Amnesty International estimated the number of displaced at over one million.

The influx sparked an outbreak of ethnic violence in Karachi between the city's Muhajir, who are the descendants of original refugees from India, and the Pashtun, who include the recent immigrants from the Northwest provinces. In 2011, over 1,000 people were killed during intermittent clashes between political parties representing the city's Pashtun population and those representing the Muhajirs or Urdu-speaking population.

Karachi had another mark against it: it was the initiation point for NATO supplies being shipped to US troops in Afghanistan. That meant the city also experienced serious political unrest as protesters of drone attacks and the US occupation of Afghanistan tried to block the NATO shipment routes from the city's port.

So we can see in the case of Pakistan the ripple effects of drone warfare. The direct casualties caused by the attacks feed into the political unrest and bloody ethnic warfare in Karachi that is exacerbated by the hundreds of thousands of refugees pouring into the city. The large-scale structural problems caused by drone warfare will likely persist for years, even after the United States and NATO forces have pulled out of the region. At its heart, the plight of refugees in the already poor, under-resourced and conflict-ridden city of Karachi represents the second tier of catastrophe caused by a form of warfare repeatedly and consistently presented as the cost-free magic wand that can eliminate terror.

Meanwhile, as the drone attacks in Pakistan continued to wreak havoc, US officials announced near the end of 2011 that the number of 'high-value' Al Qaeda targets in Pakistan had dwindled to two.[236]

US drone attacks have also claimed innocent victims in Afghanistan, Iraq, Yemen, Somalia and Libya. Like in Pakistan, their stories are usually buried along with their bodies. Even the drone killing of an American teenager elicited little discussion.

Sixteen-year-old Abdurahman Anwar al-Awlaki was born in Denver, but left for Yemen with his family in 2002. The teenager's Facebook page showed him as a typical, smiling teenager with glasses who liked rap, hip-hop, and swimming.[237] Not so typical, however, was his father, Anwar al-Awlaki, one of Al Qaeda's prominent propagandists.

The Awlaki family moved from the United States to Yemen in 2002. Abdurahman lived with his mother in the capital Sanaa. According to his mother, the teenager ran away from home in October 2011 to try to find his father. A week later, he was killed in a drone attack.

If the killing of a sixteen-year-old American fails to spark any substantial debate in the American media regarding the blatantly extrajudicial nature of drone attacks, then certainly the killing of poor Yemenis or Somalis is not going to cause a stir.

The United States is not the only country killing by remote control. A report published in the *Washington Post* in December 2011 detailed the Israeli military's use of drone aircraft over the Gaza strip, where millions of Palestinians live in crowded quarters. The misery of their existence is exacerbated by the fear—and buzzing—of being constantly watched and suddenly targeted by unmanned aircraft.[238]

In 2009, Human Rights Watch relayed numerous reports of drones hitting civilians during the 2009 Israeli invasion of Gaza. In one case, a mother was sitting on the roof while her small son Mu'mim rode a bicycle. Suddenly, there was a powerful explosion. When Nahla Allaw managed to see through the dust and smoke, she looked at her son in horror. 'His legs were crushed, his chest had tiny holes in it, and blood poured from them. I carried him, crying. He was breathing his last breath. I talked to him, saying, "It's alright my dear."'[239]

The Palestinian Center for Human Rights reported that missiles fired by the drones have led to 825 deaths, with a large percentage of those killed being civilians who perished because they were mistakenly targeted or because of the shower of shrapnel from the strikes themselves. With the American public lulled by the rhetoric that calls killing terrorists a necessity for national security and ignores the cries of victims rendered silent by the chokehold of local complicity and imperial might, the drone war represents one of the greatest travesties of justice in our age. Not only does it execute American citizens and innocent civilians with impunity, it renders hundreds of thousands of others maimed psychologically, left homeless and without a livelihood.

For Americans, these unaccounted-for acts of aggression represent an erosion of democracy. Declarations of war are no longer determined by elected officials acting on behalf of the American people, but by unknown, anonymous contractors and government assassins who kill with regularity but face no requirement of responding to those Americans, you and I, in whose name they so easily, effortlessly, press the 'shoot' button.

6

Murder by Drone: Is It Legal?

'If you do something for long enough, the world will accept it. The whole of international law is now based on the notion that an act that is forbidden today becomes permissible if executed by enough countries.... International law progresses through violations. We invented the targeted assassination thesis and we had to push it. At first there were protrusions that made it hard to insert easily into the legal moulds. Eight years later it is in the center of the bounds of legitimacy.'

—Colonel Daniel Reisner, former head of the Israeli Defense Forces Legal Department[240]

'We're not in kindergarten on this anymore: we've been doing this [targeted killings] since 2001, and there's a well-established protocol.'

—Bruce Riedel, former CIA officer[241]

It used to be that if the US government wanted someone in a foreign land dead, it would simply deploy elite assassins who would use everything from exploding cigars to good old-fashioned bullets to eliminate their target. But knocking someone off in person carried with it significant risks, both for the would-be assassin, who could be killed or captured, as well as those ordering the hit, who could at the very least be shamed—and perhaps even indicted.

But times have changed. Now when it comes to carrying out state-sponsored assassinations, the US government prefers the ease and comfort of an unmanned drone strike under the legal auspices of its global war on terror. Beginning under the administration of President George W. Bush, the reliance on drones for extrajudicial killings has since soared under his successor, with President Barack Obama employing them not just in Iraq and Afghanistan, but also far from any battlefield where the US is officially at war.

In Pakistan, a nominal US ally, Obama authorized four times as many drone strikes in just his first two years in office as his predecessor approved in two full terms. Regardless of who has been in the White House, though, the excuse has always been the same: the strikes are exercises in self-defense.

Indeed, under both Republican and Democratic administrations, US officials have insisted that the government has the right to assassinate anyone, anywhere, who they believe poses a threat to America. The US government need not be formally at war with any country in which it carries out those killings, nor need it present any evidence—in a civilian trial, a military tribunal or the court of public opinion—that the target has committed a crime. In fact, in the vast majority of cases, according to the *Los Angeles Times*, the US government does not even know the identities of those whom it is slaughtering.

This was not the case. Three times in recent history—under Gerald Ford, Jimmy Carter, and Ronald Reagan—presidents have issued orders making it illegal for anyone employed by or acting on behalf of the US government to engage in, or conspire to engage in, assassination.

In fact, just two months before the 9/11 attacks, the US ambassador to Israel, Martin Indyk, denounced Israel's targeted killing of Palestinians. 'The United States government is very clearly on record as against targeted assassinations,' he said. 'They are extrajudicial killings, and we do not support that.'[242]

But President Bush lifted the twenty-five-year ban on US assassinations just before 9/11. The practices the US government chastised Israel for were soon embraced as part of the American war on terror. And nobody in the government called it assassination anymore.

The presumption of innocence, jury trials and formal declarations of war became bothersome legal anachronisms. American presidents now assert the right to be judge, juror and executioner, a *de facto* license to kill free from the irksome interference of checks and balances. The only law that really matters is 'the Law of 9/11.'

As far as domestic law is concerned, the legal underpinning for drone attacks is the 2001 Authorization for the Use of Military Force (AUMF), which the US

Congress passed just one week after 9/11. It empowers the president to 'use all necessary and appropriate force' to pursue those responsible for the terrorist attacks. The National Defense Authorization Act of 2012 reaffirmed the president's authority under the 2001 authorization.

At a March 2010 address at the American Society of International Law, the Obama administration's top legal adviser, Harold Koh, attempted to counter increasingly loud criticism that extrajudicial killing by drones violates international norms.[243] 'The United States is in an armed conflict with Al Qaeda as well as the Taliban and associated forces, in response to the horrific 9/11 attacks,' Koh said, 'and may use force consistent with its inherent right to self-defense under international law,' including 'lethal operations conducted with the use of unmanned aerial vehicles.' But many legal experts take issue with Koh's sweeping statement, and the policies it justifies.

WHAT IS THIS 'RIGHT TO SELF-DEFENSE'?

Under international law, all nations possess the right to defend themselves against an imminent attack. For instance, if an army is amassing troops along one's border in clear preparation for an invasion, that nation is legally entitled to act in 'anticipatory' self-defense. But, as the US government itself maintained during a landmark case in the 19th century that helped establish the international precedent, such an act is only justified if 'the necessity of that self-defense is instant, overwhelming, and leaving no choice of means, and no moment of deliberation.'[244]

In other words, a country's political leaders can't

legally employ lethal force simply because, maybe, at some indeterminate point in the future, they believe an individual or nation could decide to do them harm. That's why the 2003 invasion of Iraq, which the Bush administration claimed was an act of 'pre-emptive' self-defense, was a clear violation of international law, as even the Pentagon's own Richard Perle conceded.[245] Saddam Hussein may have been a repressive dictator, but there was never any evidence he had either the intention or capability of striking the US homeland.

The drone wars are, perhaps even more brazenly, in defiance of the law. There are two types of drone strikes. 'Personality strikes' are where a specific person is being targeted because he has been placed on a 'kill list' for being deemed a threat to the United States. The second type, called 'signature strikes,' are based not on the presence of a known terrorist suspect sworn to the destruction of America, but on whether the targeted person's or persons' 'pattern of life' fits that of a militant in the eyes of a drone operator thousands of miles away. These strikes target groups of men who bear certain signatures, or defining characteristics associated with terrorist activity, but whose identities are not known. To make matters worse, the government has refused to say what those 'defining characteristics' are. Despite the murkiness, most drone strikes fall into this second category.

Even when the US government was killing armed combatants, it's not clear these attacks are actually eliminating threats to America. Most of the Taliban based in Afghanistan and Pakistan, for instance, have sought to drive foreign occupation forces out of their homeland, not launch international terror attacks.

The same goes for militants in Somalia. In 2011, the Obama administration began using Predator drones there to strike at suspected members of the Al Shabab militia, a group that aims to create an Islamic state and is currently warring against the Western-backed—and unelected—government of the country.[246] While no one would confuse its members with non-violent peace activists, the group is not a threat to the US homeland. The Obama administration even admitted that. As the *Washington Post* reported in December 2011, the US military's Joint Special Operations Command (JSOC) had for some time been chomping at the bit to increase the number of drone strikes in Somalia, including against Al Shabab camps where US citizens are known to have gone for training.[247] 'But the administration has allowed only a handful of strikes,' the paper reported, 'out of concern that a broader campaign could turn al-Shabab from a regional menace into an adversary determined to carry out attacks on US soil.'

In other words, the Obama administration conceded that Al Shabab did not pose a threat to the United States—and that only a broad and sustained drone strike campaign could change that. So much for drones only being deployed for self-defense. As it turns out, even the US government acknowledges that their use threatens to increase the risk of attacks on America.

WHO ARE LEGITIMATE TARGETS?

Even if someone is whipping up anti-American sentiment or advocating jihad against the West, can you legally kill them for that? No. There are rules about whom you can target.[248] If you are in an armed conflict, targeted killing is legal if and only if the target is a 'combatant,' a 'fighter' or, in the case of a civilian, someone who 'directly participates in hostilities.' The phrase 'direct participation' means someone who directly supports combat—that is, has a gun or a bomb in his hands—or who is actively planning or directing future military operations. It is not someone who only planned operations in the past, or someone who provides financial support, advocacy or other non-combat aid.

When you are *not* in an armed conflict, the rules are even stricter. The killing must be necessary to protect life and there must be no other means, such as capture or nonlethal incapacitation, to prevent that threat to life.

Deciding what is a legitimate target is particularly difficult when the US is engaged in a part of the world where its understanding is limited and intelligence is so often faulty. Time and again, drones have targeted the wrong house or the wrong group—from wedding parties to meetings of tribal elders.

We know the government makes mistakes, lots of them, in giving people a 'terrorist' label. During the Bush administration, former Defense Secretary Donald Rumsfeld assured the public that the prisoners locked up in Guantánamo were all 'the worst of the worst,' only to find out that hundreds were innocent people who had been sold to the US military by bounty hunters. Why should the public believe what the Obama administration says about the people being assassinated by drones?

WHAT ABOUT THOSE DOUBLE TAPS?

It seems clear that the US has, on numerous occasions, targeted a site multiple times in quick succession, a practice known as 'double tap.' A February 2012 report by the Bureau of Investigative Journalism found that from January 2009 until January 2012, at least fifty civilians were killed in follow-up strikes when they had gone to help victims.[249]

Secondary strikes have discouraged people from helping the wounded, and even inhibited the provision of emergency medical assistance from humanitarian workers.

An individual known pseudonymously as Hayatullah Ayoub Khan, interviewed by 'Living Under Drones' researchers, recounted a particularly harrowing incident. While driving in Waziristan, a missile was fired at a car about 300 meters in front of him. When he got out of his car and approached the wreckage, he saw an arm moving inside the crushed vehicle. The wounded man in the car yelled that he should leave immediately because another missile would likely strike. Khan started to return to his car when a second missile hit and killed the wounded person. He said that nearby villagers waited another twenty minutes before removing the bodies, which included the body of a teacher from his village.

The threat of the 'double tap' also affects professional

humanitarian workers. One humanitarian organization told researchers they had a policy to wait for six hours before going to the site of a reported drone strike.

Legal experts say that the 'double tap' strikes on first responders violates international humanitarian law's basic rules of distinction, proportionality, and precautions. It also violates specific legal protections for medical and humanitarian personnel, and for the wounded.[250]

Christof Heyns, the UN special rapporteur on extrajudicial executions, said, 'If civilian rescuers are indeed being intentionally targeted, there is no doubt about the law: those strikes are a war crime.'[251]

CAN A GOVERNMENT KILL ITS OWN CITIZENS WITHOUT TRIAL?

On September 30, 2011, a US Predator drone flying over Yemen fired a Hellfire missile at a car carrying two American citizens, Samir Khan and Anwar al-Awlaki. Both were propagandists for a terrorist group that took its inspiration from Al Qaeda. Samir Khan was the editor of *Insight*, an English-language propaganda magazine for Al Qaeda in the Arabian Peninsula, and was not on the 'hit list.' He was merely collateral damage in the US attack on al-Awlaki, a radical Muslim cleric who had been placed on a secret assassination list more than a year earlier.

The Obama administration never deigned to present any evidence against al-Awlaki. The reasons he was placed on a presidential kill list are classified. No evidence implicating al-Awlaki in acts of terrorism—as opposed to giving unpopular speeches—was ever released to the public and he was never so much as charged with a crime. The Obama Justice Department even fought attempts by his father aimed at compelling the government to do just that. But the court sided with the administration, calling the president's decision to order the assassination of an American citizen, with no due process or explanation, 'judicially unreviewable.'

The judge's decision left serious questions unanswered. Outside of the context of armed conflict, shouldn't the government only be allowed to carry out the 'targeted killing' of an American citizen as a last resort to address an imminent threat to life or physical safety? Why didn't the court order the government to disclose the legal standard it uses to place US citizens on government kill lists? Why is judicial approval required when the United States decides to target a US citizen overseas for electronic surveillance, but not required when the government decides to target a US citizen overseas for death?

'If the court's ruling is correct, the government has unreviewable authority to carry out the targeted killing of any American, anywhere, whom the president deems to be a threat to the nation,' said Jameel Jaffer, Deputy Legal Director of the ACLU. 'It would be difficult to conceive of a proposition more inconsistent with the Constitution or more dangerous to American liberty. It's worth remembering that the power that the court invests in the president today will be available not just in this case but in future cases, and not just to the current president but to every future president. It is a profound mistake to allow this unparalleled power to be exercised free from the checks and balances that apply in every other context.'[252]

Immediately following al-Awlaki's death, President Barack Obama announced that the assassination was 'a major blow' against Al Qaeda. Representative Peter King, chairman of the House Homeland Security Committee, insisted the lethal strike was lawful. 'It was entirely legal,' he said. 'If a citizen takes up arms against his own country, he becomes an enemy of the country.'

But like any other American citizen, al-Awlaki was entitled under US law to a presumption of innocence and jury trial, even if it had to be *in absentia*. Al-Awlaki may have been a traitor who had defected to the enemy, but the Constitution requires that he be convicted on the 'testimony of two witnesses' or a 'confession in open court,' not the say-so of the executive branch.

Since al-Awlaki—like many other never-charged terrorist suspects taken out in targeted killings—was not in an active war zone, under international law the US government ought to have exhausted all attempts to capture and detain him before resorting to lethal force. The Obama administration refused to do that, indicating that lethal force is the government's first resort, not its last.

After the killing of al-Awlaki, lawmakers, policy experts and former government officials spanning the political spectrum argued for more transparency around the US drone program.[253]

Instead of transparency, the CIA responded two weeks later with another drone strike in southeastern Yemen that killed nine people, including al-Awlaki's sixteen-year-old American son. US officials say those who gave the order to kill did not know the American teenager was in the group. But even if they had known, it's not clear they would have stopped the attack, and no disciplinary measures were taken against those who authorized the strike that killed a young American who posed no threat to the United States.

WHY NOT CAPTURE TERROR SUSPECTS?

Under the Bush administration, hundreds of people labeled 'enemy combatants' were rounded up far from the battlefield and imprisoned—for indefinite terms without charge or trial—at Guantánamo Bay and in prisons in Iraq and Afghanistan. The CIA captured and detained hundreds more at black sites around the world. This proved to be problematic. Legal experts denounced indefinite detention as an affront to international norms, and many of those detained were indisputably innocent. This left the US government with a long-term public relations nightmare, exacerbated by the inhumane, torturous conditions described by those it wrongfully imprisoned.

Barack Obama was determined not to make the same mistake. His counter-terrorism policy was markedly different from that of his predecessor, but not exactly the way human rights activists would have wished. Some called it the kill-don't-capture doctrine.

Noah Feldman, a constitutional and international law professor at Harvard University, put it this way: 'Obama's team observed that holding terror suspects exposed the

Bush administration to harsh criticism (including their own).'[254] By contrast, 'Dead terrorists tell no tales—and they also have no lawyers shouting about their human rights.'

The kill-don't-capture Obama doctrine was bluntly explained by Attorney General Eric Holder during a March 2010 congressional hearing.[255] Asked about the possibility of affording Osama bin Laden a trial, he responded that the questioner was 'talking about a hypothetical that will never occur. We will be reading Miranda rights to the corpse of Osama bin Laden.'[256]

In a mission aided by surveillance drones, an unarmed bin Laden was killed by a team of Navy SEALs, which the *National Journal* noted 'wasn't an accident.'[257]

'A high-ranking military officer briefed on the assault said the SEALs knew their mission was not to take him alive,' the *Journal* reported.

The lesson of Guantánamo Bay and the Bush years appears to be this: extrajudicially killing alleged terrorists—while just as legally dubious—is superior to detaining them. It precludes the possibility of long-term international embarrassment and public campaigns by uppity human rights activists. And no one, not even members of a military tribunal, need assess the evidentiary basis for the killing.

CAN THE US CARRY OUT DRONE ATTACKS ANYWHERE IT WANTS?

No. In a May 2010 report, Philip Alston, an expert on international law at New York University who was then the United Nations' Special Rapporteur on Extrajudicial, Summary or Arbitrary Executions, was clear. 'Outside the context of armed conflict, the use of drones for targeted killing is almost never likely to be legal.'[258]

The United States, the most prolific user of drones to carry out targeted killings, asserts its attacks are legally justified as it is engaged in a global war against Al Qaeda and associated terrorist groups. By this rationale, the CIA would be justified in dropping a Hellfire missile on a suspected terrorist in an apartment in Hamburg, a restaurant in London or a mosque in upstate New York. Why stop at merely dropping bombs in poor countries dominated by people of color?

Alston's report noted that the broad US claim of a global armed conflict skirts some of the most central legal issues, including: 'the scope of the armed conflict in which the US asserts it is engaged, the criteria for individuals who may be targeted and killed, the existence of any substantive or procedural safeguards to ensure the legality and accuracy of killings, and the existence of accountability mechanisms.'

Most troubling, said Alston, is that the US government has 'refused to disclose who has been killed, for what reason, and with what collateral consequences. The result has been the displacement of clear legal standards with a vaguely defined license to kill, and the creation of a major accountability vacuum.'

Other experts concur. 'Drones are not lawful for use outside combat zones,' Mary Ellen O'Connell, a professor at Notre Dame Law School, testified at an April 2010

Congressional hearing. 'Outside such zones, police are the proper law enforcement agents and police are generally required to warn before using lethal force.'[259]

Translation: While the US government asserts that its war on terror is global in scope, armed conflict is real and legally definable. If a military is fighting in an actual battle on an actual battlefield, then, no, it legally need not arrest and charge enemy fighters. But far away from a firefight in a recognized war zone, law enforcement, not militaries or intelligence agencies, is the appropriate—and legal—tool for pursuing those alleged to have ties to terrorism. That means that outside the context of a real battlefield, it is illegal to use weaponized drones, which are weapons of war incapable of taking a suspect alive.

As the ACLU put it in an April 2010 letter to President Obama, 'The entire world is not a war zone, and wartime tactics that may be permitted on the battlefields in Afghanistan and Iraq cannot be deployed anywhere in the world where a terrorism suspect happens to be located.'[260]

BUT WHAT IF A COUNTRY CONSENTS TO DRONE STRIKES?

Some argue that drone strikes outside recognized war zones are legal if the governments in whose territory they take place have offered their consent. In these cases, the argument goes, one cannot claim national sovereignty has been violated.

According to a leaked US State Department cable, the thirty-three-year dictator of Yemen, President Ali Abdullah Saleh, agreed to allow drones and other American aircraft to launch strikes within his country, famously saying, 'We'll continue saying the bombs are ours, not yours.'[261] Saleh was ousted by a popular uprising in 2011, and the new leader, President Abed Rabbo Mansour Hadi, went even further to please the US, publicly admitting that he personally approves every drone strike.

The position of the Pakistani government has been more complicated. At first, they consented privately but made public condemnations. A US diplomatic cable released by WikiLeaks quoted Prime Minister Yousuf Gilani saying, 'I don't care if they do it as long as they get the right people. We'll protest in the National Assembly and then ignore it.'[262] In late 2011, even that tacit consent was withdrawn after a NATO airstrike mistakenly killed twenty-four Pakistani soldiers.[263] The Pakistani government responded by evicting a CIA drone base near its border with Afghanistan and threatening to shoot down any drones that violated its airspace. While the government never shot down a drone, Pakistani officials did become more and more vocal about their opposition to the strikes, calling them unlawful, counterproductive, and a violation of the nation's sovereignty.[264]

Legally, however, it doesn't really matter whether a government consents or not. Sovereignty is but one aspect of the legal argument against extrajudicial drone killings. Another is the right of the accused. While some governments may have given the green-light for drone strikes within their territories, Professor O'Connell noted in her congressional testimony that they 'cannot, however, give consent to a right they do not have.' Just because a foreign leader gives the okay for a foreign government to kill one of its citizens does not make it legal, in other words. Indeed, 'States may not use military force against individuals on their territory when law enforcement measures are appropriate.'

WHO HAS THE RIGHT TO CARRY OUT THESE ATTACKS?

Outside of an active war zone, no one has the right under international law to launch a drone strike. Within a war zone, however, uniformed military personnel—and only uniformed military personnel—are legally entitled to employ lethal force, a fact the US government has itself cited in order to declare its Taliban opponents in Afghanistan 'unlawful combatants.'

While the US Air Force and JSOC have been conducting many drone operations, the CIA, a civilian agency, has played a significant role. According to Gary Solis, a law professor at Georgetown University and author of *The Laws of Armed Conflict*, that is plainly illegal.

'In terms of international armed conflict, those CIA agents are, unlike their military counterparts but like the fighters they target, unlawful combatants,' Solis wrote in a March 2010 Op-Ed in the *Washington Post*.[265] 'No less than their insurgent targets, they are fighters without uniforms or insignia, directly participating in hostilities, employing armed force contrary to the laws and customs of war. Even if they are sitting in Langley, the CIA pilots are civilians violating the requirement of distinction, a core concept of armed conflict, as they directly participate in hostilities.'

And it's not just CIA agents violating the law. The *New*

York Times reported in August 2009 that the CIA's drones are in fact armed by private contractors from Blackwater, or 'Academi' as it's now known.[266] And information obtained by McClatchy-Tribune News Service under the Freedom of Information Act found that at least a dozen defense contractors supply personnel for all aspects of the drone program, including in the so-called kill chain before missiles are launched.[267]

Writing in a military law journal in 2008, Lt. Col. Duane Thompson, chief lawyer for the Air Force Operations Law Division, warned that allowing non-military personnel to communicate targeting information directly to pilots would violate international laws of war.[268]

Civilians are not subject to the Uniform Code of Military Justice, which holds military personnel accountable for war crimes or for violations of rules of engagement on the use of force. 'Persons who relay target identification for an imminent real-world mission to persons causing actual harm to enemy personnel or equipment should be uniformed military,' Thompson wrote.

WHAT IF A COUNTRY OTHER THAN THE UNITED STATES DID IT?

Proponents of American exceptionalism believe that what America does is right just because it is America doing it. But other than by pointing to George Washington and the red, white and blue, it will be hard for defenders of the US's extrajudicial drone killings to make a principled case against other countries assuming the right to unilaterally launch drone strikes against their perceived enemies.

That was the warning delivered in an October 2011 statement by Christof Heyns, the United Nations' Special Rapporteur on extrajudicial, summary or arbitrary executions.[269] An expert on human rights law based at the University of Pretoria in South Africa, Heyns strongly cautioned against the use of extrajudicial death-by-drone, noting that the 'use of such methods by some States to eliminate opponents in countries around the world raises the question why other States should not engage in the same practices.'

That America is America and thus entitled to employ tactics not permitted of less exceptional nations might work as an argument on a Sunday morning talk show or on the *Washington Post* editorial page. But out in the real world, Heyns noted, 'The danger is one of a global war without borders, in which no one is safe.'

As Human Rights Watch points out, were the US rationale to be applied by other countries, China might declare an ethnic Uighur activist living in New York City as an 'enemy combatant' and send a missile into Manhattan; Russia could assert that it was legal for them to fatally poison someone living in London whom they claim is linked to Chechen militants.[270]

Or consider the case of Luis Posada Carrilles, a Cuban-American living in Miami who is a known terrorist.[271] Convicted of masterminding a 1976 bombing of a Cuban airliner that killed seventy-three people, Posada has openly admitted to carrying out acts of terrorism with the express goal of overthrowing the Cuban government, including a spate of bombings in Havana in the 1990s (one of which killed an Italian tourist). In 2000, he was arrested in Panama with more than 30 pounds of C-4 explosives and accused of plotting to assassinate Fidel Castro as he addressed hundreds of students at the University of Panama. Pardoned four years later, Posada illegally entered the United States.

Given the precedent set by the US government with its targeted killings abroad, the Cuban government could claim—particularly in light of the failure of the US legal system to bring Posada to justice—that it has the right to drop a Hellfire missile in downtown Miami to take out an admitted terrorist and sworn enemy.

That would not make it right. But just as the US's employment of torture undermines its authority to denounce torture elsewhere, so it goes with its use of drones to assassinate perceived enemies. While exceptionalists may defend America's right to employ such techniques, the prospect of other nations using that precedent ought to give them pause.

WHAT ABOUT CIVILIAN CASUALTIES?

A key concept in international conflict law is proportionality. This means that you have to weigh the importance of the military target against the harm that might come to civilians during the action, and you have to do everything possible to prevent mistakes and minimize civilian casualties.

In present-day warfare, soldiers are not duking it out on the battlefield but fighting in urban and rural settings teeming with residential houses, bustling markets, children playing, pedestrians walking. The combatants the Americans are fighting don't wear uniforms, and many are soldiers by night, farmers or taxi drivers or some other profession by day. The biggest problem is not so much fighting the enemy as *finding* the enemy.

That's where drones come in. But while their super-sensitive cameras can spot the guy carrying explosives and launch a missile to 'neutralize' him, all too often those missiles also take out the car driver or family members or casual passersby.

Luis Moreno-Ocampo, Chief Prosecutor at the International Criminal Court, wrote that 'international humanitarian law and the Rome Statute permit belligerents to carry out proportionate attacks against military objectives, even when it is known that some civilian deaths or injuries will occur. A crime occurs if there is an intentional attack directed against civilians or an attack is launched on a military objective in the knowledge that the incidental civilian injuries would be clearly excessive in relation to the anticipated military advantage.'[272]

The key question, then, is who gets to define 'excessive'? If a missile hits its target but also takes out one innocent person, is that excessive? If it takes out two innocents for the one enemy, is that excessive? Three? Who is to say? And even more important, is anyone even asking these questions?

In the absence of enough inquiring voices, and wrapped in the cloak of legal ambiguity and national security, impunity reigns.

It wasn't until March 2012 that Attorney General Eric Holder, speaking to law students at Northwestern University School of Law, addressed these legal issues. He said the Constitution empowered the President to protect the nation from any imminent threat of violent attack, and that there were no geographic limitations because 'we are at war with a stateless enemy, prone to shifting operations from country to country.' He went on to justify killing even US citizens in foreign countries because the Constitution does not guarantee its citizens the right to judicial process, but only 'due process.' The best response to Holder came not from the legal community, but from TV comedy host Stephen Colbert.

'Yes, the founders weren't picky,' Colbert agreed. 'Trial by jury; trial by fire; rock, paper, scissors. Who cares? Due process just means there is a process that you do.' The current process, he explained, is that the president meets with his advisors and decides whom to kill. Then he kills them. 'If we're going to win our never-ending war against terror, there are bound to be casualties,' Colbert sighed, 'and one of them just happens to be the Constitution.'

7

Morality Bites the Dust

'The drones were terrifying. From the ground, it is impossible to determine who or what they are tracking as they circle overhead. The buzz of a distant propeller is a constant reminder of imminent death. Drones fire missiles that travel faster than the speed of sound. A drone's victim never hears the missile that kills him.'

—David Rohde, kidnapped by the Taliban in 2009[273]

Some say drones save lives—and not just those of pilots. Drone proponents say they save the lives of soldiers thanks to the critical air support they provide to the ground troops, and they save civilians in conflict zones because they are more precise than high aerial bombing or long-range artillery. And, they argue, if you can kill the leaders of a violent extremist group with precision bombs and therefore prevent a wider conflict, it's the moral thing to do.

That was certainly the consensus during a meeting I had with representatives of the State Department and the Pentagon. 'There's a war going on, and drones are the most refined, accurate and humane way to fight it,' said Jeff Hawkins from the US State Department's Democracy and Human Rights Bureau. When asked about the anti-American backlash, he replied, 'I spent three years in Pakistan. There are so many conspiracy theories and so much anti-American sentiment in that country anyway. If it wasn't the drones, they'd simply be angry at the United States for something else.'

Maureen White, who deals with refugees at the State Department and was previously on the board of Human Rights Watch, was enthusiastic about drones and insisted that the real problem was one of marketing. 'We have failed to control the debate,' she said. 'The Taliban have a home-grown movement in the tribal areas of Pakistan that is vicious. They are terrorizing civilians and creating thousands of refugees. Taking out the leaders with drones is critical. It's a pinpointed, targeted, precise and successful mechanism. From a military standpoint, drones are a dream come true.'

The reality, however, is more complex. For while drones make it easier to kill some bad guys, they also make it easier to go to war.

During the war in Vietnam, every family with a draft-age son was affected. So were their friends, their girlfriends, their grandparents—basically the whole community, at least among those who couldn't buy their way out of military service. The same was true during World War II, when millions of Americans served in the military and those who didn't were largely involved in support activities. Today, however, there is no obligatory military service and less than 1 percent of the population is enlisted.

Fewer Americans are serving and, thankfully, fewer Americans are dying in today's wars. While the death of every US soldier is a terrible tragedy, US deaths in post-9/11 wars are a fraction of those in previous conflicts, in part because of improvements in medical care. Over 400,000 American soldiers were killed in World War II and over 50,000 in Vietnam, compared with just over six thousand in the decade of wars in Afghanistan and Iraq from 2001–2011. One consequence of lower enlistment and lower casualties, however, is that there has been less of a national sense of urgency to examine whether the wars are worth fighting.

The economic crisis that began in 2008 led to greater questioning of whether America could afford such a huge Pentagon budget and eroded public support for US military involvement in Afghanistan and Iraq. But it was not high up on the list of issues Americans—millions of whom were out of work—cared about. So Congress was able to keep allocating money for war, year after year, against the wishes of the majority.

With drones substituting more and more for boots on the ground, the conflicts become even more obscure. The paradox is that while the US military is engaged in more and longer conflicts than ever in our history, fewer people are involved, touched, concerned, or engaged. The public is barely even aware of these conflicts. It's like a low-grade fever that the body politic has learned to live with and basically ignores.

'Robots may entail a dark irony,' warns philosopher Peter Singer.[274] 'By appearing to lower the human costs of war, they may seduce us into more wars.'

Drones may be but the latest tool for killing and certainly not worse than, say, an atomic bomb. But the casual ease with which they can be used, in contrast to a nuclear weapon, threatens to make war all the easier. And that is a problem, according to Yosef Lapid, a professor of international relations at New Mexico State University, which is an hour away from the premier US training site for drone pilots at Holloman Air Force Base.[275] It's one thing if drones are 'reducing the number of casualties or the risks that soldiers are assuming on the battleground,' Lapid told the *GlobalPost*. But 'if that means killing becomes facile or societies have less problem engaging in war, then it's a very serious problem.'

With drone warfare, there is no need to unite the country behind a conflict, no need to call for shared sacrifice, no need for grueling debates in Congress. That was certainly the case with President Obama's decision to get involved militarily in the overthrow of the regime of Libyan leader Muammar Qaddafi.

On March 17, 2011, the United Nations Security Council passed Resolution 1973 sanctioning the establishment of a no-fly zone and the use of 'all means necessary' to protect civilians within Libya.[276] Just weeks later, President Obama approved the use of Predator drones, armed with Hellfire missiles, to pound Qaddafi's compound and his loyalist troops. Six months later, Qaddafi was captured and killed. While the National Transitional Council nominally took control, warlords, Islamists, tribal leaders and would-be democrats were all vying for power.

President Obama authorized the use of force in Libya without going to Congress. He insisted that he didn't need Congressional approval, since it was only an air war and the US was not sending troops. In a report to Congress, the administration claimed that US military operations in Libya were consistent with the War Powers Resolution and did not require congressional authorization because US military operations are distinct from the kind of hostilities contemplated by the Resolution.[277] 'US operations [in Libya] do not involve sustained fighting or active exchanges of fire with hostile forces, nor do they involve the presence of US ground troops, US casualties or a serious threat thereof.'[278]

US operations didn't involve 'sustained fighting,' 'active exchanges of fire' or a 'serious threat' of US casualties because the fighting was done by drones. Libyan ground forces couldn't exchange fire with machines that targeted them from 50,000 feet. And they couldn't kill pilots who weren't there. While congresspeople on both sides of the aisle refuted this argument, the administration didn't budge—and there were no legal consequences.

US involvement in Libya set a precedent for a bizarre definition of war that only applies if US troops are being put at risk. This is a clear example of 'war made easy,' lowering the threshold for future US interventions by presidential decree.

The Libya campaign was also dangerous for two other reasons. It reinforced the notion that high-tech air strikes are free of civilian casualties. 'We have carried out this operation very carefully, without confirmed civilian casualties,' claimed NATO Secretary General Anders Fogh Rasmussen.[279] It took *New York Times* reporters to refute this claim, with an incomplete on-the-ground examination revealing dozens of civilians killed by air strikes, including at least twenty-nine women or children, often asleep in their homes when the ordnance hit. The US and NATO refused to acknowledge mistakes or compensate victims, as they have been forced to do in Afghanistan.

The Libya example also reinforces the notion that high-tech weapons spell success, which is not always the case. It was true enough in Libya—without NATO air cover, it's unclear whether the rebels on the ground would have achieved victory. And in the case of Libya, the air strikes were supporting a popular uprising. But one should never forget the lessons of the US disaster in Vietnam or the folly of the Soviet occupation in Afghanistan. History is replete with examples of poor guerrilla armies, with the crudest of weapons, defeating sophisticated foreign invaders because the former were fighting for a cause they truly believed in.

Technological advantages can be quickly rolled back when the other side creatively adapts, which they tend to do. A case in point is the American Revolution, when the greatest military power in the world was defeated by a ragtag army employing guerrilla warfare. Another example is Iraqi fighters responding to US heavy vehicles by planting simple roadside bombs, or Hezbollah responding to Israeli drones by acquiring drones of their own.

One of the problems of relying on high-tech weapons is not just that they can create a false sense of superiority, but that they also create a built-in incentive to use them. After spending many millions on purchasing and training personnel for a new weapons system, the military is anxious to test the weapons in real combat. Those who received the training want to test their skills. And of course the arms manufacturers are anxious to see their weapons used, so that more and more will be bought.

Some of the private contractors who are hired to participate in the CIA's drone program have another incentive. Joshua Foust of the American Security Project discovered that in some targeting programs, contracted staffers have review quotas—that is, they must review a certain number of possible targets per given length of time. 'Because they are contractors, their continued employment depends on their ability to satisfy the stated performance metrics,' Foust explained.[280] 'So they have a financial incentive to make life-or-death decisions about possible kill targets just to stay employed. This should be an intolerable situation, but because the system lacks transparency or outside review it is almost impossible to monitor or alter.'

A policy paper on UAVs by the United Kingdom's Ministry of Defence asked questions rarely heard in US government circles. 'If we remove the risk of loss [of our soldiers] from the decision-makers' calculations when considering crisis management options, do we make the use of armed force more attractive? Will decision-makers resort to war as a policy option far sooner than previously?' The document goes on to suggest, albeit in a convoluted way, that one of the reasons for foreign military interventions in Pakistan and Yemen is precisely the availability of drones. 'That these activities are exclusively carried out by unmanned aircraft, even though very capable manned aircraft are available, and that the use of ground troops in harm's way has been avoided, suggests that the use of force is totally a function of the existence of an unmanned capability—it is unlikely a similar scale of force would be used if this capability were not available.'[281]

Pakistan would never have allowed manned aircraft in its airspace, just like it won't allow foreign combat troops in its territory. Precisely because drones are unmanned, the Pakistani government felt that this was a way to placate the American government while at the same time providing a pretext to its own people that somehow its sovereignty wasn't being violated.

In the United States, this tendency to use force is sanctioned by a population that lives in a state of fear. Ever since 9/11, the public has been subjected to a concerted, massive propagation of fear that has become so common as to be unnoticeable, except perhaps when asked to remove your shoes by airport security. Public fear of terrorism is routinely inflamed and amplified by politicians, including President Obama, through never-ending references to 9/11.

The official government acceptance of unlimited

detention of US citizens in the passage of the National Defense Authorization Act (NDAA), and the backing by many politicians of Guantánamo detention and torture, finds support in public fear of terrorism. These policies also reinforce that fear by affirming that these gross denials of human rights are made necessary by monstrous and numerous enemies we are supposedly facing. And it allows the government, in a society that prides itself on being the world's greatest democracy, to commit gross violations of traditional rules of human conduct, such as international laws, which are norms born out of huge wells of human suffering through decades of war.

People are more likely to speak out against state-sponsored violence when their fears are countered by another basic human instinct: empathy for those being injured and killed. But since 9/11, the US government and mass media, whether by specific agreement or unspoken understanding, have systematically deprived the US public of images of the dead and wounded in war that would evoke feelings of empathy. Pictures of torture from Abu Ghraib did appear, but others remain secret. For years, even coffins of dead US soldiers could not be photographed. And although thousands of people have been killed and maimed by drone attacks, the American public has yet to see photographs or video from the aftermath of these strikes. Pakistani photographer Noor Behran has photographed hundreds of drone victims. While his photos appear in media outlets all over the world, there is a virtual blackout in the US media.

During the Vietnam War, it was different. Certainly, the

draft and the deaths of large numbers of US soldiers fed the anti-war movement. But as the war dragged on, Americans began to see and learn more about the Vietnamese and their treatment at the hands of US troops. 'We see the rice fields of a small Asian country being trampled at will and burned at whim,' roared Martin Luther King Jr. in his famous 1967 address. 'We see grief stricken mothers with crying babies clutched in their arms as they watch their little huts burst forth into flames.'

Today, rather than exposing the public to the horrors of war, drones make war look fun—at least for those firing the missiles. YouTube has hundreds of video clips of combat footage from Iraq and Afghanistan, much of it captured by drones, which are themselves flown using a controller modeled after the Playstation.

The Defense Department itself began putting up mission clips on YouTube as a way of promoting drones domestically and intimidating the enemy. The ability to download videos of combat footage to home computers and iPhones turns war into a form of entertainment. Soldiers call these clips 'war porn' and they have been a smash hit, with well over ten million views.

Video clips showing Americans blowing up some anonymous, faceless enemy reinforces racist stereotypes of 'poor bastards' who deserve to 'get toasted,' such as these comments posted by online viewers of a video from Afghanistan called 'Hell is coming for breakfast': 'They better pre-order some of them virgins for these murderous terrorist jihadists!' Or, 'Kill em all and let God sort em out!'

Another video, set to techno music, shows an Iraqi being blown up. 'Great video! Rock on America. Where can I get the music?' wrote one viewer. 'Hold on while I get some popcorn. I want to see more of the barbarians blown up,' another joked.

'Our side,' the civilized culture, is the one with the high-tech killing machines. Their side is barbaric because they still kill using old-fashioned methods, including knives. A jihadist cutting off his enemy's head is gut-wrenching. But is it worse than pressing a button to kill the enemy from afar, and perhaps an entire family besides? 'People are a lot more comfortable with a Predator strike that kills many people than with a throat-slitting that kills one, but mechanized killing is still killing,' said former CIA lawyer Vicki Divoll.[282]

When leaders of Hamas were criticized for launching crudely made rockets into Israel that terrorized civilians, one leader said, 'If we had the high-tech weapons the Israelis have, we could target our missiles to hit Israeli military bases and not civilians. But we don't have them.'[283]

Some ethicists and religious leaders argue that drone warfare is a particularly morally bankrupt way of waging war, that it violates the precepts of just war theory to fight in a way that shields one from the mortal consequences. When military operations are conducted through the filter of a far-away video camera, there is no possibility of making eye contact with the enemy and fully realizing the human cost of an attack.

In 2003, the Defense Department developed a new

computer program that was supposed to give the military a better sense of the human cost of an attack. It is an intricate program that shows how much damage would be caused by a particular bomb dropped by a particular aircraft flying at a particular altitude. The dead show up as blob-like images resembling squashed insects, which is why the program was called 'Bugsplat.' Bugsplat also became the 'in-house' slang referring to drone deaths; 'squirters' is slang for people scurrying away trying to flee the attacks. While dead people and terrified people running for their lives might look like bugs from on high, such references certainly don't inspire a reverence for life.

The *Christian Century*, a leading Protestant magazine, editorialized that while the drone attacks have no doubt killed terrorists and leaders of Al Qaeda, 'they raise troubling questions to those committed to the just war principle that civilians should never be targeted.'[284] Taking aim at one of the aspects of drone warfare that make it so popular with the military and with politicians—that it is a risk-free option for the US military because it avoids American casualties—the *Century* editors said: 'According to the just war principles, it is better to risk the lives of one's own combatants than the lives of enemy noncombatants.'

Saving the lives of 'enemy noncombatants' does not seem to be very high on the list of priorities for the US government and many Americans, including liberal ones. Witness this shocking exchange between conservative commentator Joe Scarborough and liberal Joe Klein:

> *Scarborough: [Drones] are focused on killing the bad guys, but it is indiscriminate as to other people who are around them ... You do it with a joystick in California, and it seems so antiseptic, it seems so clean, and yet you have 4-year-old girls being blown to bits because we have a policy that now says: Instead of trying to go in and take the risk and get the terrorists out of hiding in a Karachi suburb, we're just going to blow up everyone around them ...*
>
> *Klein: The bottom line in the end is—whose 4-year-old gets killed? What we're doing is limiting the possibility that 4-year-olds here will get killed by indiscriminate acts of terror.*

Of course, killing children in Waziristan makes it more likely, not less likely, that someone will try to kill children in Washington. As to the moral bankruptcy of justifying the murder of innocents, constitutional lawyer Glenn Greenwald compared the twisted thinking of America's Joe Kleins to that of Al Qaeda and the Taliban. 'To the extent one wanted to distinguish them,' said Greenwald, 'one could say that the violence and aggression brought by the US to the Muslim world vastly exceeds—vastly—the violence and aggression brought by the Muslim world to the US. That's just a fact.'[285]

Some suggest that if the US military really wants to protect civilians, it should not use drones but ground troops, who are more capable of discriminating between innocent bystanders and militants. While invading countries risk significantly higher casualties by deploying troops, this is precisely what the logic of just war requires.

In the magazine *Christianity Today*, founded by evangelical minister Billy Graham, author and president emeritus of Trinity Episcopal School for Ministry Paul F. M. Zahl went even further in his critique of drones, accusing them of 'emasculating the enemy.'[286]

'I use *emasculate* intentionally, because our victims live in societies where male humiliation is a fate almost worse than death,' wrote Zahl. Snipers in the sky reduce people on the ground to a condition of absolute helplessness, because they cannot fight back against unmanned drones. 'This is not a David versus Goliath scenario,' he wrote. 'It is a case of the Philistines telling the Israelites that they are not even permitted to put a champion on the field.' While this might appear to be a good strategy, he maintained that it instills a lifetime desire for revenge, 'birthed from one "silver glint" way up in the sky that kills without warning or recourse.'

That 'silver glint' way up in the sky, killing without warning or recourse, is in the process of becoming even more distant. Pretty soon, drones could also end up killing autonomously, without any sort of direct human input. 'You can envision unmanned systems doing just about any mission we do today,' one Air Force engineer told *Popular Science*.[287] Based on recent tests by the military, the *Washington Post* predicts that the future of the American way of war could be drones that 'hunt, identify and kill the enemy based on calculations made by software, not decisions made by humans.'[288] Human traits such as commonsense and compassion, all too absent from wars as it is, could become nonexistent in 21st century conflicts.

The path towards autonomy is a slippery slope. First comes autonomous take-off and navigation, then target selection, then killing the target without human intervention. While Pentagon officials insist that a human being will remain somewhere in the loop, their role will be minor. 'Humans will no longer be "in the loop" but rather "on the loop," monitoring the execution of certain decisions,' said robotics expert Noel Sharkey. 'Simultaneously, advances in artificial intelligence will enable systems to make combat decisions without human input.'[289]

While Sharkey is horrified by this notion, Ronald Arkin of the Georgia Institute of Technology's Mobile Robot Laboratory thinks it's grand. 'Robots are already stronger, faster and smarter,' he explained in an interview with *Popular Science*. Arkin has designed an 'ethical governor' for drones that he argued could abide by the laws of war better than a living, breathing soldier. 'Why wouldn't they be more humane? In warfare where humans commit atrocities, this is relatively low-hanging fruit.' Presumably Arkin has never watched 'Terminator' or 'The Matrix.'

Whether machines can ever be 'more humane' than the humans that program them is a dubious notion. While human beings do indeed commit atrocities when caught up in the heat of war, they sometimes also empathize with the supposed enemy. A World War II study by US Army Brigadier General S.L.A. Marshall interviewing thousands of soldiers found that the majority of troops refused to fire their weapons at other human beings. S.L.A. Marshall's methodology has been criticized, but his findings have been corroborated by many other studies.[290] Indeed, data indicate that soldiers throughout military history have demonstrated a strong resistance to killing other people. Drones, one can safely assume, would not be so resistant.

Worse yet, autonomous robots cannot discriminate between combatants and non-combatants. The laws of war say that belligerents may not attack civilians, wounded soldiers, the sick, the mentally ill, or captives. 'There are no visual or sensing systems for robots that are up to that challenge,' said Sharkey. 'The Geneva Convention requires soldiers to use common sense. But computers have no common sense. How can they be ethical when they have no means of distinguishing grandmothers from soldiers?'

War has always been a powerful incentive for technological innovation. Now technology is on the verge of supplanting the human soldier altogether—with consequences we can barely imagine.

8

The Activists Strike Back

KIRK: Yes, Councilman, you have a real war on your hands. You can either wage it with real weapons, or you might consider an alternative. Put an end to it. Make peace.

ANAN: There can be no peace. Don't you see? We're a killer species. It's instinctive.

KIRK: But the instinct can be fought. We're human beings with the blood of a million savage years on our hands, but we can stop it. We can admit that we're killers, but we're not going to kill today. That's all it takes. Knowing that we won't kill today.

—Star Trek

You may not have heard of the 'Creech 14,' but they have a special place in the heart of the anti-drone movement. If you saw a photo of the group, you might think they had just walked out of Sunday mass; indeed, some of its members are priests and nuns. But whether clergy or not, all are spiritually rooted in a theology that calls on people of faith to stand up against injustice—in deeds, not just words.

And so, on April 9, 2009, the group of fourteen activists entered Creech Air Force base—where teams of young soldiers remotely operate many of America's killer drones—protesting what they considered war crimes taking place inside. As they crossed onto the base, the group invited staff nearby to share a Good Friday meal with them. They were then told to leave, and when they refused, they were arrested, charged with trespassing and held in jail until Easter Sunday.

While the action was noteworthy, the most remarkable part was not anything that took place that day, but the trial itself, which did not begin until over a year later, on September 14, 2010, at the Clark County Regional Court in Las Vegas, Nevada. There, the defendants turned what would have been a mundane case over a minor misdemeanor into a broad debate about the use of drones. They decided not to be represented by lawyers but to represent themselves. They also invited three expert witnesses to speak on their behalf: Ramsey Clark, who was US Attorney General under President Lyndon Johnson; Center for Constitutional Rights legal director Bill Quigley; and retired Army colonel Ann Wright.

The defendants took turns questioning the witnesses, establishing the fact that drone strikes kill a large number of civilians; that people have the right, even the duty, to stop war crimes; and that according to the post-World

War II Nuremberg principles, individuals are morally and legally bound to disobey orders that entail crimes against humanity. They cited the history of protesters who broke petty laws, from the nation's founders to the Suffragists to the civil rights activists who illegally sat in at lunch counters. 'In the long run, we honor them for obeying a higher law, for helping to bring us toward justice,' said Quigley.[291]

In a surprising turn of events, at the end of the trial, Judge Jansen declared that the issues at stake were too important to make an immediate ruling and gave himself four months to analyze the case. On January 27, 2011, the judge handed down his twenty-page decision. He found the group guilty of the crime of trespassing, concluding that they had been unable to prove their conduct was compelled by true 'necessity.' But he gave the defendants credit for the time they had already spent in jail and declared them free to go. 'Go in peace,' were Jansen's final words.

While the defendants were hoping for a non-guilty verdict, they knew they had won a victory no matter the ultimate ruling. As defendant Brian Terrell said in his closing statement, 'Some have noted that the trend toward using drones in warfare is a paradigm shift that can be compared to what happened when an atomic bomb was first used to destroy the city of Hiroshima in Japan. When Hiroshima was bombed, though, the whole world knew that everything had changed. Today everything is changing, but it goes almost without notice. I hesitate to claim credit for it, but there is certainly more discussion of this issue after we were arrested for trespassing at Creech Air Force Base on April 9, 2009, than there was before.'[292]

The transcript of that trial was so riveting that it was later turned into a play that is being used by religious groups as an educational tool. And the Creech 14 inspired similar protests, including one clear across the country in upstate New York.

On April 22, 2011, over three hundred activists organized by the local Upstate Coalition to Ground the Drones and End the Wars descended upon the Air National Guard Base at Hancock Field in Syracuse, New York. They chose the location because the National Guard at the base had been remotely flying weaponized Reaper drones over Afghanistan since late 2009.

As they approached the entrance, thirty-eight of them—two in wheelchairs—draped themselves in white cloth splattered with fake blood and dropped to the ground, a dramatic 'die-in' intended to represent civilians killed in drone attacks. Dozens of police rushed in to intervene. After protesters refused to get up, they were forcibly removed in handcuffs.

The 'Hancock 38,' as they came to be known, were charged with obstruction of traffic and disorderly conduct. When they went to court on November 3, 2011, they, too, got former US Attorney General Ramsey Clark to testify on their behalf. Clark insisted that drones inherently violate the laws of the United States and international law, and that the crimes the Hancock 38 had been charged with paled in comparison to the crimes the defendants were trying to stop.

Outside the courthouse, dozens of people staged a mock drone attack, complete with a three-dimensional drone model, someone 'manning' the drone from behind a computer, civilian victims covered in fake blood and a man labeled 'Al Qaeda Recruiter' who was using the deaths to gain more recruits.

The final verdict of the case was delivered on December 1, 2011. Judge Gideon found the defendants guilty on two charges of disorderly conduct, with sentences ranging from fines and community service to the maximum penalty of fifteen days in jail. The judge admitted that he had spent 'many a sleepless night' before making his decision and that he learned a great deal during the five-day non-jury trial. 'Ultimately, the defendants have arguably accomplished that which they sought by their actions—the drawing of acute attention to their message,' he concluded.

The Creech 14 and the Hancock 38 are just two examples of the growing US protest movement against the use of drones. In Pakistan and Yemen, people are pouring out into the streets by the thousands to condemn drone attacks that have devastated their communities. But in the US and Europe, where the effects of the drones are hidden from public view, activists have been slowly shaping the foundation of an anti-drone movement. By 2012, the No Drones Network had recorded protests in eighteen states. Still in its early stages, the movement lacks clear strategies with tangible goals. But as it evolves, it may well prove to be as successful as earlier campaigns to ban landmines and cluster bombs.

One of the few American peace activists who have traveled dozens of times to Iraq and Afghanistan is Kathy Kelly, co-coordinator of Voices for Creative Nonviolence. During a trip to Afghanistan, Kelly wrote this report:

> *I met with a large family living in a wretched refugee camp. They had fled their homes in the San Gin district of the Helmand Province after a drone attack killed a mother there and her five children. The woman's husband showed us photos of his children's bloodied corpses. His niece, Juma Gul, age nine, had survived the attack. She and I huddled next to each other inside a hut made of mud on a chilly December morning. Juma Gul's father stooped in front of us and gently unzipped her jacket, showing me that his daughter's arm had been amputated by shrapnel when the US missile hit their home in San Gin. Next to Juma Gul was her brother, whose leg had been mangled in the attack. He apparently has no access to adequate medical care and experiences constant pain.*[293]

Back in the 1980s, when the US government was funding and arming right-wing death squads in Central America, one of the strategies the peace movement employed was to organize hundreds of delegations to the region. Through these direct experiences, thousands of people became educated on the injustices being funded with their tax dollars and became motivated to do something about it. Returning delegates formed the heart and soul of the peace movement. But those trips to Central America were quick, inexpensive and relatively safe.

Trips to places like Afghanistan and Iraq are costly and dangerous.

Despite the dangers, Voices for Creative Nonviolence organizes delegations to Afghanistan because they know how important it is to create a core of committed activists with firsthand knowledge. Kelly's colleague Brian Terrell recalls how profoundly he was impacted when, on one of the Afghan trips, he met a nine-year-old girl who had lost her arm in a drone attack. 'That still haunts me,' Terrell said. 'Drones are predators armed with Hellfire missiles, and the concept that peace could come from these killing machines is ridiculous.'[294]

Unlike Kelly, Nancy Mancias has never been to those places halfway across the world where the US is unleashing its killer drones, but this has not dampened her resolve. Mancias runs the Ground the Drones campaign for the peace group that I co-founded, CODEPINK. As a passionate anti-war advocate, Mancias has been actively trying to bring the troops home from their overseas misadventures. She has also been part of the movement against torture and a proponent of closing the prison in Guantánamo, as well as a fierce believer in accountability for war crimes. She alerts people around the country when war criminals like George Bush or Dick Cheney will be speaking, encouraging them to try to make a citizen's arrest or at the very least some ruckus—the latter being something Mancias herself is famous for.

Like many in the anti-war movement, Mancias views her work against drones as a natural extension of her efforts to promote peace. 'The troops may come home from

Iraq and Afghanistan, but drone attacks for extrajudicial assassinations will likely continue throughout the Middle East, Central Asia and Northern Africa. That's why it's so critical to draw attention to drones and build a movement to stop them,' she said. Mancias collaborates in creative actions and public forums with groups like Voices for Creative Nonviolence, Nevada Desert Experience, Syracuse Peace Council, Catholic Workers, Pace e Bene, and others across the United States.

Another well-known activist focusing on drones is Jim Haber, who became involved in the movement after he found himself living near Creech Air Force Base. In 2008, Haber moved to Las Vegas to take a job with Nevada Desert Experience, an anti-nuclear organization that has been part of the movement against nuclear weapons testing since the early 1980s. He realized that every time he traveled from Las Vegas to the Nevada Test Site, he passed by one of the key hubs for operating UAVs around the world. 'I couldn't pass Creech Air Force Base and not do anything about what goes on there—or rather, what is controlled from there,' said Haber. 'So I started articulating the connection between drones and antinuclear work, pointing out that nuclear weapons are the chronic underpinning of US military projection while drones and other emerging robotic weapons are the acute forces in use today.'

Haber is also connected to the Catholic Worker movement, a group of communities around the United States dedicated to helping the poor and practicing nonviolent resistance against injustice. Many Catholic

Workers feel that resisting drones is part of their spiritual commitment. That's true for Mary Anne Grady and two of her sisters. All three were a part of the Hancock 38 group that got arrested for protesting drones in upstate New York. 'The Bible says that all life is sacred,' said Grady. 'We need to expose the use of drones and the expansion of militarism, which does not respect the sacredness of life.'

It's not only seasoned activists and religious communities taking a stand against drones. Even veteran government officials have come forward. Retired CIA analyst Ray McGovern is one of the most outspoken critics of drones. He is a frequent commentator on TV, railing against drone warfare and the civilian casualties they cause. McGovern not only gives talks, writes articles and blogs, he joins protests and gets arrested for his convictions.

So does retired US Army Colonel Ann Wright. While her home is in beautiful Honolulu, Hawaii, Wright generally lives out of a suitcase, traveling the country speaking out about the need for peace, always making a point to educate her audiences about the dangers of drones. And like McGovern, she doesn't just speak out: she puts her body on the line, racking up so many arrests that her profile is on a FBI criminal database.

Activists in other countries, such as Britain and Sweden, have also become involved in the anti-drone movement, many prompted by their own countries' complicity in the use of UAVs in Afghanistan and elsewhere. Agneta Norberg, a Swedish activist with the group Women for Peace, started protesting drones when she discovered that

Sweden had purchased UAVs from Israel and was training drone pilots in Sweden. Appalled, in October 2011 she helped organize the Swedish Peace Council's conference on drones and joins others to vigil in front of Parliament.

In England, groups such as Fellowship of Reconciliation, England, and Women in Black regularly hold vigils. Helen John, a decades-long campaigner against nuclear weapons, now keeps vigil at the Royal Air Force base at Waddington, UK, where drone pilots are located. But she doesn't just keep vigil. The 73-year-old activist has camped outside the Waddington base for weeks at a time, and has cut holes in the fence and broken inside. Nonviolent confrontation and improvisation, she believes, can turn tiny protests into big, influential ones. 'I don't believe in the use of any weaponry, but there is something quite noble about someone who is prepared to lay down their life [in combat],' John told a reporter. 'But sitting in an air-conditioned room thousands of miles away...killing by remote control. These weapons are a complete departure from civilised behaviour. That's why we need to stir up as many problems as possible for this place,' she added, referring to the air force base.[295]

The Nevada Desert Experience, Voices for Creative Nonviolence, Nevada County Peace Center, CODEPINK and others in the US hold vigils at least once a month outside US air bases.

Activists target bases for two reasons: First, they have the chance to interact with military personnel as they hand out information to people in their cars entering and leaving the base. Sometimes they even get a chance to interact with the soldiers who operate the drones, reminding them of their commitment to the rule of law and their obligation not to follow illegal orders. Second, having a presence at a base also informs the local community. It's hard for folks living or commuting past the bases to miss the protesters' messages, which come in the form of anything from large, colorful banners to lifelike model drones. Activists also invite the press to join them, hoping to reach a broader audience.

Debra Sweet, the director of the anti-war group The World Can't Wait, suggests reaching out to a different audience: students at middle schools and high schools. Sweet visits students to talk to them about the wars and warn students that the government is on the prowl for video game geeks they can recruit to operate drones. She often brings along Iraq and Afghanistan war vets from the group We Are Not Your Soldiers to share personal testimonies.

Some activists have taken their message to public venues that glorify war, like the drone exhibit at the Smithsonian Air and Space Museum in Washington, DC. In January 2010, a group called Peace of the Action—started by anti-war activist Cindy Sheehan, who lost her son in the war in Iraq—entered the museum and dropped a banner next to the drone exhibit reading: DRONES KILL KIDS. A few months later, they not only unfurled a massive, multi-story banner that read DRONES: VIDEO GAME FOR US, BLOOD-BATH FOR THEM, but they also dropped hundreds of fliers explaining why they opposed drones, fliers that floated through the air into the hands of the unsuspecting tourists below.

Organizer Nick Mottern also takes his anti-drone message to public venues, but he brings along a special home-made prop: an eight-foot-long model drone with an eleven-foot wingspan that floats through the air perched atop a ten-foot-high sheet rock lifter rolling on oversized wheels. People passing by stop in their tracks and ask questions, providing a window of opportunity to discuss robotic warfare. 'Throughout my entire anti-war activist career, dating back to the Gulf War, I have never seen a sign or prop cause so much curiosity and interest,' said Mottern.

Now retired and living in Westchester, New York, Mottern was first inspired to make the drones when he discovered that one of the companies in his community, ITT Corporation, manufactures the bomb releases on Predator drones. Outraged, Mottern suggested staging a war profiteers march near the house of CEO Steven Loranger. Wanting to visually convey the trauma of drone terrorism to Loranger, Mottern built the model drone. The media loved it, publishing several pictures in the local paper.

Since then Mottern and his colleagues have made several models, displaying them to audiences around the country as they give talks on robotic warfare. In October 2011 they made a guest appearance at Occupy Wall Street in New York City's Financial District, and later in an anti-drone demonstration at a General Atomics building in Washington, DC. They are such a hit that activists as far away as Australia have contacted them asking how to make models for their own protests.

Mottern's next move is to install video cameras in the nose of the drones, setting a computer next to them so people can get a taste of what it's like to have drones watching their every move.

Activist Jean Aguerre is not trying to educate people about drone warfare; she's trying to keep drones out of her community. Aguerre grew up on a ranch in southeast Colorado near the Comanche National Grasslands—land that had been reclaimed from the devastating Dust Bowl back in the 1930s. For thirty years, local residents have been fighting back against the military's expansion into this delicate bioregion, but the fight has intensified with the advent of drones because the Army has its eye set on seizing 6.9 million acres of shortgrass prairie for unmanned aerial development, low altitude flights and robotic weaponry testing.

The military acquisition would take up 94,000 square miles of mostly private property, displacing thousands of Coloradans. And the civilian airspace for a robotic flight zone would reach across state lines, across sovereign indigenous nations, across national parks. It would extend as far north as Aspen, Colorado and as far south as Albuquerque, New Mexico.[296]

Aguerre's group, the Not 1 More Acre campaign, has taken a firm stand against the proposal and in 2007 achieved an overwhelming bipartisan vote in Congress to ban funding for any activity related to expanding the site. They have motivated people across the nation to petition Congress, successfully renewing the ban each year since. To keep tabs on what the government is up to, campaigners often send in Freedom of Information Act requests that reveal the government's plans, contracts and activities advancing the military takeover of southern Colorado and northern New Mexico, including the last intact shortgrass prairie remaining in the American Great Plains.

Activists around the country have also begun targeting the places where the drones are made and the people who are receiving multimillion-dollar contracts to produce them.[297]

In April 2010 a group called the Alliance to Resist Robotic Warfare and Society (ARROWS) organized a conference called 'Challenging Robotic Warfare and Social Control.' Held in Columbia River Gorge, Oregon, near the Boeing corporation's military drone complex, it brought together over 125 people from veterans' groups, churches, and peace organizations throughout the US Northwest. The conference ended with a protest at Boeing's ScanEagle drone headquarters.

One of the most popular targets for direct actions is dronemaker extraordinaire General Atomics. Numerous protests have taken place at their offices, but some activists have gone even further—paying a visit to the home of their CEO, James Neal Blue.

On May 18, 2010, my colleagues at CODEPINK held a somber vigil outside the CEO's elegant residence in La Jolla, California. They arrived at 10 a.m. to find several news vans and police cars waiting for them. Unfurling banners that read, 'Drone Attacks = Terror,' the protesters set up a small altar with roses and candles to commemorate the children killed in drone attacks.

The next day, they organized the first-ever protest outside the General Atomics corporate headquarters in San Diego. News of the vigil at James Blue's house the day before had spread quickly, and members of the community informed the activists that some of the General Atomics employees had decided to stay home to avoid the attention. But the company's leadership had also gone through the trouble and expense of renting a 7-foot-high chain-link fence to surround the headquarters' entire perimeter. They were certainly afraid of a handful of peaceful protesters!

When the peace activists began arriving at 7:30 a.m., they 'beautified' the rent-a-fence by adding roses and banners with messages like 'Stop Drone Attacks' and 'General Atomics, Your Profits = Civilian Deaths.'

Within an hour, some sixty protesters had gathered. They carried signs, peace flags and model drone planes to make sure their presence was understood by General Atomics employees and any passersby. 'Our intent was simply to ask the employees to think about the company they work for and hold the management accountable for the killing machines they manufacture,' Nancy Mancias explained.

The protesters laid down for a die-in, and chalked the outlines of their bodies to leave behind a representation of the civilians killed indiscriminately by drone attacks. Three protesters then sat down in the driveway, preventing any access to the property and creating a backup of cars along the road. The police attempted to negotiate with them. 'What do we want? We want General Atomics to agree to stop making drones,' the protesters insisted. Since the police couldn't deliver that, the group then asked to meet with CEO James Neal Blue, a meeting they had already requested weeks in advance. The police couldn't arrange that either. So the sit-in continued.

After over an hour of preventing access to the company's headquarters and more than four hours of disrupting business as usual, CODEPINK, San Diego Peace Resource Center, and the coalition of activists packed up.

'This is one morning when we made it difficult to get to work,' Mancias commented, 'but there are mornings in Pakistan and Afghanistan when people never make it to work at all, or arrive to find buildings and roads destroyed by US attacks.'

By 2012 there were weekly protests outside the headquarters of General Atomics organized by San Diego Veterans for Peace, and a coalition of peace groups was calling for a yearly national mobilization in San Diego to shine a spotlight on the company responsible for producing the killer drones.

Sometimes activists have targeted 'secondary companies,' i.e., those that have relationships with firms involved in the drone-making business. These can be easier targets because they may have more of a public face than weapons companies, and because it might be easier for them to sever their partnerships. In early 2011, CODEPINK contacted the car company Nissan to protest the relationship between Nissan and AeroVironment. AeroVironment makes the charging system for Nissan's electric car, the Leaf, but it also makes a variety of small drones. Nissan portrays itself as part of the green movement, as exemplified by their electric car, but here they were partnering with a company involved in drone warfare. CODEPINK asked Nissan to cut its ties with AeroVironment, but got no response.

So a group of Los Angeles activists decided to crash the Nissan exhibit at the prestigious LA auto show. They jumped onto the Leaf's platform, chanting, unfurling banners and calling upon Nissan to stop supporting drone warfare. They were eventually escorted off the premises, but not before getting out their message and embarrassing the company.

One of the best ways to build an activist base is to focus on local connections to drone warfare. Fran Quigley, a professor, lawyer, and journalist, had been researching the disturbing trend of robotic warfare and decided to see if his home state of Indiana was involved.

After submitting several Freedom of Information Act (FOIA) applications, he was surprised at the number of connections he uncovered. In West Lafayette, a company called Lite Machines had a multimillion-dollar contract with the Navy to manufacture a mini-drone. Rolls Royce in Indianapolis was making the engines for the Global Hawk. In Indianapolis, battery maker EnerDel had a $4 million contract to make batteries for drones. The engineering faculty at Purdue was doing research on drones, as was the Naval Surface Warfare Center in south central Indiana. And in Terre Haute, the Air National Guard was helping to pinpoint targets for drone attacks in Afghanistan and Pakistan. 'There's nothing special about Indiana in this field,' said Quigley, 'so I presume that if you did the research, you'd find significant drone activities going on in universities, small factories and research parks all across the country.'

'Our state needs jobs, but I hate the fact that people of good conscience may be sucked into the military-industrial complex process of creating machines that contribute to the death of innocent civilians,' said Lori Perdue, an Air Force veteran and Indiana member of CODEPINK. 'If we could create green jobs instead of war jobs, I bet the guy working the line making jet turbines would rather be building a wind turbine.'

Quigley and the local activists have been educating students and plan to organize demonstrations outside the drone warfare support sites.

A group in Iowa didn't even wait until the local factory started working on drones to protest. As soon as they got wind that a company called AirCover Integrated Solutions was going to partner with the University of Iowa to build small surveillance drones in Cedar Rapids, they began protesting.[298] Company President James Hill said the protesters were misdirected, that the drones would be used for good purposes like searching for people lost after earthquakes, finding wandering patients with dementia and looking for suspicious packages in stadiums.[299]

But protesters think the drones will really be used to spy on the public, including folks like themselves. 'The prospect of having drones flying around, spying on people, is kind of horrific,' said Nate Adeyemi, one of the local organizers. 'It's such an infringement upon the human right to privacy.' The group is also protesting the university for its involvement and the local officials who gave the company a loan.

Another target for activists has been the organization that lobbies on behalf of the industry, the Association for Unmanned Vehicle Systems International (AUVSI). The group was created in 1978 'to promote and support the unmanned systems and robotics industry.' The organization has ballooned to include 1,400 members—all anxious to feed at the government trough. Activists have crashed their press conferences, conventions and fairs.

Given their close connections in Congress—the companies give millions in campaign contributions and get, in return, billions of tax dollars—AUVSI can even show off its wares right inside the Capitol. At an exhibit hosted by the Congressional Drone Caucus in September 2011, activists broke up the lovefest, unfurling white sheets covered in fake blood and falling to the floor, moaning and writhing in pain. 'Stop the killer drones,' they wailed, while another protester carrying a large cardboard drone made a loud buzzing noise as he zoomed around the room. Startled, the congresspeople, staffers and corporate employees were forced to stop their conversations—until the police arrived and escorted the group out of the building.

While protesters are busy naming and shaming companies, some of the nation's best legal and human rights groups have been taking the issue of drone warfare and extrajudicial assassinations to court. The Center for Constitutional Rights (CCR) and the American Civil Liberties Union (ACLU) sued Treasury Secretary Tim Geithner over the government's decision to put US citizen Anwar al-Awlaki on a hit list and freeze his US assets. They brought the case to a US federal court on behalf of Anwar al-Awlaki's father, hoping to prevent the targeted killing of his son.[300]

They lost the case on procedural grounds, but the judge was disturbed by the 'serious questions' raised by the practice. 'Can the executive order the assassination of a US citizen without first affording him any form of judicial process whatsoever, based on the mere assertion that he is a dangerous member of a terrorist organization?' the judge inquired.[301]

The UK-based human rights law group Reprieve is bringing litigation against some European governments that have been complicit in the drone attacks on their nationals, including the governments of the UK, Germany, Belgium, France, and Spain. The laws in Europe make it easier than in the United States to sue in the courts. 'We're going to sue the government in Britain because the British have admitted that they provide intelligence for the drone attacks,' said Reprieve director Clive Stafford Smith. 'I think we have every chance to find violations of Geneva Conventions and humanitarian law. Whether we win in court or not, though, it's the kind of thing where the British government cannot prevail in the court of public opinion, as what they are doing is just wrong.'

Reprieve assisted its Pakistani partner organization,

Foundation for Fundamental Rights, to lodge a legal case in Pakistan against John Rizzo, the former acting CIA general counsel who gave the final okay for adding names to the CIA's hit list, and against the CIA station chief in Pakistan, Jonathan Banks, who fled the country after he was named in the case. The group is also investigating UK corporations involved in the production of drones for possible lawsuits.

Another US group, the Electronic Frontier Foundation (EFF) has filed lawsuits about drones, but their focus is the secrecy surrounding the domestic use of drones. EFF filed a suit demanding that the Federal Aviation Association release data on certifications and authorizations the agency has issued for the operation of unmanned aircraft. Certification by the FAA is required to operate a drone over 400 feet. And though the FAA said there were 285 certifications covering eighty-five different users as of mid-September 2011, the details on those users were unclear.

The EFF is publicly listing the information it receives from the FAA. It is also asking people around the country to contact their police departments with questions about their use or intentions to use drones, and collecting this information in a national database.

Jennifer Lynch, the staff attorney for EFF, said that the use of drones domestically was raising significant privacy concerns. 'Drones give the government and other unmanned aircraft operators a powerful new surveillance tool to gather extensive and intrusive data on Americans' movements and activities,' she said. 'As the government begins to make policy decisions about the use of these aircraft, the public needs to know more about how and why these drones are being used to surveil United States citizens.'[302] Other groups are insisting that if the FAA does not protect people's privacy, then Congress should enact additional protections.

Human Rights Watch has taken on an even more difficult task: trying to get more transparency and accountability for the CIA's secret drone program. It has called on the Justice Department to release information such as legal memos on targeted killings, drone videotapes from specific attacks, and after-action reports. Where there is a finding of wrongdoing, the group says, individuals responsible for conducting or ordering unlawful attacks should be promptly investigated and disciplined or prosecuted.

Human Rights Watch also thinks the drone program should be taken out of the hands of the CIA. Since the US government is unwilling to demonstrate that the agency is abiding by international legal requirements for accountability and redress, the group feels the use of lethal drones should be exclusively within the command responsibility of the US military.[303]

This was echoed by professor Mary Ellen O'Connell in her testimony to Congress in April 2010. 'Restricting drones to the battlefield is the most important single rule governing their use,' she said, adding that at the very time the United States was trying to win hearts and minds to respect the rule of law, 'we are ourselves failing to respect a very basic rule: remote weapons belong on the battlefield.'[304]

The American Civil Liberties Union wants the

government to account for casualties. Through a Freedom of Information Act request, the ACLU received an official statement from the Department of Defense confirming it does not compile statistics about the total number of civilians killed or injured by drones. 'Given widespread concerns about drone warfare and varying estimates of civilians killed, the Defense Department should compile data about the number of civilian casualties caused by drones and disseminate that information to the public,' said Jonathan Manes, an attorney with the ACLU National Security Project.[305]

The Center for Civilians in Conflict agrees. It asserts that good military practice to minimize civilian harm dictates data collection before, during and after a combat operation, analysis of any harm that occurs and a review of lessons learned. But the Center goes farther, calling on the government to not only keep a record of civilians harmed by US drones, but also to compensate them. In 2010 the Center released a report called 'Civilian Harm and Conflict in Northwest Pakistan,' showing that there was no comprehensive or systematic accounting of drone strike casualties nor any measure of amends, including compensation, for civilian victims.[306]

'There are US systems in place, imperfect as they are, to compensate an Afghan harmed by a US convoy or small arms fire. But not a Pakistani harmed by a drone. Why are their losses treated differently?' asked the Center's Executive Director Sarah Holewinski. 'This makes no sense, and worse, it disrespects civilians, leaving them to suffer with no recognition or help.'[307]

Holewinski told me that her group has tried repeatedly to meet with the CIA, but has had no success. 'There's a Catch 22, which is that the program is secret, it "doesn't exist." So how can they meet to talk about a program that doesn't exist?'

It is precisely where this 'non-existent' CIA program operates, Pakistan, where the largest outpouring of anti-drone protests have occurred. These include tens of thousands rallying in Peshawar and Karachi, hundreds sitting down on the main highway between Pakistan and Afghanistan to physically block the NATO supply route, general strikes in North Waziristan and protests outside Parliament in Islamabad.

The immensely popular Pakistani opposition leader and former cricket champion Imran Khan has led the nation's largest rallies against drone strikes. In October 2012, Khan and thousands of his followers organized a caravan to Waziristan to rally against the drones. A CODEPINK delegation of thirty-two Americans joined them and spent time in Pakistan meeting with drone victims, the US embassy, military leaders, lawyers, women's groups, and human rights organizations. They also held a fast in downtown Islamabad to commemorate the lives of innocent drone victims.

The delegation received an enthusiastic welcome from Pakistanis and helped develop cross-border ties. They also returned home charged up to write, speak, and organize in their communities.

The US movement is still in its embryonic stage, with a lot of work ahead to convince the public that drones are not as precise as they are being told and are actually jeopardizing their security. But between 2010 and 2012, the movement grew tremendously. An April 2011 'Drone Summit' organized by CODEPINK in Washington DC brought together a diverse group of 500 people, from Pakistani lawyers and Yemeni human rights activists to scientists and congressional aides. The summit helped build a tighter-knit activist network.

By 2012, the anti-drone movement had grown from a handful of scattered protests to national mobilizations, waves of civil resistance at air force bases, local weekly vigils, speaking tours, die-ins, congressional briefings, webinars, e-mail lists, and activist websites. The American public had begun to wake up from its drone-induced slumber.

9

Opposition to Drones Goes Global

General, your tank is a powerful vehicle. It smashes down forests and crushes a hundred men. But it has one defect: It needs a driver.

General, your bomber is powerful. It flies faster than a storm and carries more than an elephant. But it has one defect: It needs a mechanic.

General, man is very useful. He can fly and he can kill. But he has one defect: He can think.

— Bertolt Brecht, 'From a German War Primer'

Across the Atlantic, in England, a coalition of organizations, academics and individuals emerged in 2010 called the Drone Campaign Network. Many UK groups had drones on their radar ever since the Royal Air Force started using them in 2007, but until the creation of the network, there wasn't one particular group that focused exclusively on drones.

The network is led by author and activist Chris Cole, formerly director of Fellowship of Reconciliation, Oxford. Cole helps groups connect to drone-related activities in their local area, particularly if there are manufacturers based in their communities, and organizes a yearly gathering to share information and coordinate activities. Through the blog Drone Wars UK, he keeps track of drone news, information sources, and upcoming actions.

One thing in the activists' favor is the UK public's general antipathy towards drones. After some snooping, Cole discovered on the Ministry of Defence's website that one of their top concerns was the increasingly negative public perception of drones. Suspiciously, the Ministry of Defence took down the page as soon as he publicized it on the Drone Wars UK website. 'People aren't buying the whole "they're keeping our boys safe' story," Cole said. 'With the Iraq war debacle, people are skeptical about what the military says, especially claims that the drones are so accurate that they don't kill civilians. There is also much more skepticism about the use of drones for surveillance in the UK than the US.'

The coalition includes peace groups such as War Resisters International and Campaign for Nuclear Disarmament; faith-based organizations such as Fellowship of Reconciliation, England and Pax Christi; and professionals such as Scientists for Global Responsibility. They have organized actions that range from a Stop the Arms Fair at the Houses of Parliament to demonstrations at General Atomics' new London office. Member group Child Victims of War sets up meetings with members of Parliament to complain about the number of children killed in drone attacks. Scientists for Global Responsibility disseminates information about drones on their website.[308]

The Fellowship of Reconciliation, England, which has done its own excellent reports on drone warfare, has been calling on the government to make public the number of casualties resulting from British drone attacks and calls for a more open, serious, and informed discussion about the UK's use of drones.[309] 'Drones are the latest in a long line of new weapons used in the mistaken belief that they will provide a clean and tidy solution to a conflict. Time and again history has proved that this is a myth,' their website states.[310]

The Campaign for Nuclear Disarmament Cymru (the Welsh name for Wales), or better known as CND Cymru, was inspired to speak out against drones when they discovered in 2004 that the Aberporth training area in Wales—an area that is also a missile base—was slated to become a 'UAV Centre of Excellence,' with promises to deliver one thousand jobs in an area ravaged by unemployment. Despite protests, the government went ahead with its plan. The jobs never materialized—only about thirty jobs were created—but Aberporth became one of two places in Europe where drones are flight-tested. The other location is in northern Sweden.

The group continues to raise a ruckus—holding vigils, trespassing on military property, putting pressure on their elected officials. On September 21, 2011, which is

International Peace Day, they launched a Commemorative Garden to recognize all victims of the deployment of drones. 'Quite apart from the problem that these machines and their imaging equipment were being tested over our homes, many people objected to the terrible fact that our community, and our country, was planning something appalling against people in other countries,' said CND Cymru's national secretary Jill Gough. 'We certainly don't want Wales to be part of that.'

One issue that is more prevalent in European anti-drone campaigns than American ones is the connection between Israel and the drone industry. Concerned about the occupation of Palestine and the use of drones in Gaza, UK activists were appalled to discover that their corporations were producing key components for Israeli drones, exporting them to Israel, and then buying them back in the form of completed vehicles. They are calling on their government to stop using the Israeli Hermes 450 drone made by Elbit, and to cut ties with Israeli drone manufacturers.

The Catholic peace group Pax Christi UK holds a regular vigil outside a factory called UAV Engines, also owned by Elbit.[311] Hastings Against War, a UK coalition of individuals formed in 2003 to oppose the war on Iraq, also protests against the lease and purchase of Israeli drones.[312] They are particularly vigilant around the UK Watchkeeper drone project, in which several hundred million dollars went to an Israeli company, thus indirectly supporting the occupation of Palestine.

Another approach to curbing drone warfare comes

from a group formed in 2009 called the International Committee for Robot Arms Control (ICRAC). It represents a group of robot specialists, philosophers and human rights activists from a number of countries—including the US, the UK, France, Germany, Austria, the Netherlands, and Australia.

Among the members are Noel Sharkey, a professor of artificial intelligence and robotics at the University of Sheffield; Peter Asaro, a professor of philosophy at the New School University in New York; Robert Sparrow of the Centre for Bioethics in Melbourne, Australia; and Mark Gubrud, a physicist at the University of North Carolina.

The organization started with the aim of stimulating debate about the ways that military robots have already altered the nature of warfare and subverted many of the existing rules of engagement. They were concerned that robotic technologies might tempt policymakers to think war can be less bloody, and that hostile states or terrorist organizations would be able to hack robotic systems and redirect them.

Bringing together experts from all over the world, the group held its first workshop in Berlin in the summer of 2010, organized by Jürgen Altmann, a physicist teaching at Dortmund, Germany. The meeting consisted of academics and policy experts, human rights lawyers, Red Cross representatives, peace activists, military advisers, and others opposed to the arms trade. They explored the threats to peace and international security posed by robotic weapons, including threats to civilians and the undermining of international law. In addition to worries that robots may be used as weapons in space or be armed with nuclear weapons, the experts expressed serious concerns about the inability of automated robotic systems to discriminate between combatants and civilians, and that these new technologies could make it difficult to determine the moral and legal responsibility for any atrocities committed in war.

They came up with the following goals: the prohibition of the development, deployment and use of armed autonomous unmanned systems, with the exception of automated anti-missile systems; limitations on the range of and weapons carried by 'man-in-the-loop' unmanned systems; a ban on arming unmanned systems with nuclear weapons; the prohibition of the development, deployment and use of robot space weapons; and restrictions on the use of armed drones for targeted killings in sovereign territories not at war.[313]

For guidance, ICRAC is looking back at other successful campaigns to ban certain kinds of weapons, particularly the 1997 Mine Ban Treaty outlawing the use of landmines.

After failed attempts by government institutions to regulate the use of landmines, non-governmental organizations launched their own campaign to ban the weapons altogether. In 1992, the International Campaign to Ban Landmines (ICBL) was formed, bringing together hundreds of member organizations in countries all over the world. These included organizations in both mine-producing and mine-affected countries, and groups focusing on human rights, humanitarian assistance, children, peace, disability, veterans' concerns, arms control, religious affairs, the environment, and women's issues. The members engaged in education campaigns, shared political strategies, and pushed their governments to come up with a solution.

In October 1996, fifty governments and twenty-four observers met in Ottawa to strategize, and over the course of several subsequent meetings, they drafted a treaty. The International Campaign to Ban Landmines, representing the grassroots global community, won a seat at the table—participating in all the diplomatic meetings and negotiations, helping draft the treaty, and writing the preamble to the treaty that eventually passed.[314]

The Mine Ban Treaty, officially titled the Convention on the Prohibition of the Use, Stockpiling, Production and Transfer of Anti-Personnel Mines and on Their Destruction, was adopted in September 1997. Thanks to the constant pressure from the grassroots, it was implemented in less than two years, faster than any treaty of its kind in history. By 2011, 80 percent of the world's nations had banned the use of landmines.[315]

The landmine campaign credits its success to several factors.[316]

- It had a clear message and goal. Signatory states agreed to six major commitments, among them the destruction of their mine stockpiles within four years and clearing their mine areas within ten years.
- It had a campaign structure that was non-bureaucratic and a strategy that was flexible.
- It put together an 'unusually cohesive and strategic partnership' of non-governmental organizations,

international organizations, United Nations agencies, and governments.

- There was a favorable international context.

Also critical to the campaign's success was that the negotiations took place outside the UN system, and the treaty conference relied on voting, rather than consensus, which made it easier to move forward. Governments were also required to 'opt in,' meaning that governments attending the treaty negotiation conference had to agree on the text beforehand. Strong leadership at the negotiation conference led to a persuasive treaty that was safeguarded from the possibility of governments watering it down or slowing down the negotiations.[317] Another success of the campaign was that it so stigmatized landmines that even most states that refused to sign the treaty were shamed into not using them.

Key to the fight against landmines was Jody Williams, who won the Nobel Peace Prize in 1997 for her campaign work. With the recent proliferation of unmanned aerial vehicles, Williams has been writing and speaking out against drone warfare. She would love to see a ban on all lethal drones, but she fears it would be infinitely more difficult than banning landmines because their use is already so widespread, because it's easier for the military to make the argument that their benefits outweigh their drawbacks, and most of all, because drones have become such a big business.

'I have a visceral repugnance to the use of drones; I would love for all lethal drones to disappear,' Williams said in an interview. 'But with landmines, we didn't have a lot of industry blowback because in terms of weapons sales, landmines were chump change. Drones are different. They're a cash cow for the beltway bandits. There's going to be a massive arms race for these kind of weapons and I'm afraid the companies just won't tolerate a ban.'

Even regulations on their use would be fiercely opposed by both the weapons industry and by government authorities, especially in the US. 'There would be absolutely no support in the US government for any international restrictions on the use of drones,' insisted Jeff Hawkins from the State Department's Bureau of Democracy and Human Rights at a meeting on drones. 'Of that you can be certain.'[318]

Williams thinks the best chance the international community has to curb the use of drones is to stop autonomous robotic weapons—weapons that operate independently according to pre-programmed missions—because they are not yet fully developed and because they bring up the most difficult ethical and legal questions.

'If we think it's bad now, imagine a fully autonomous vehicle going out and wiping out several villages,' said Williams. 'Who's accountable? The company who made them? The military who used them? The software developer? Perhaps they all should be taken to court but that probably isn't going to happen. So we need to stop them before they're used. And this is something I think an international coalition could accomplish.'

Peter Asaro of ICRAC agrees. He is concerned about targeted killings, but feels that these are already illegal under international law, so what is needed is enforcement, not a new treaty. In terms of a treaty banning autonomous robotic weapons, Asaro understands that there are many complex questions about implementation and enforcement, but he believes that just having an international consensus that autonomous systems are immoral and illegal would be a major step. 'An international ban would dissuade the major military technology developers by vastly shrinking the potential economic market for those systems, which would greatly slow their current pace of development,' said Asaro.[319]

Many groups agree that fully autonomous attack-and-kill robotic weapons can and must be banned before they appear in the global weapons market and fuel an entirely new and terrifying weapons race. Such a campaign is something that has the potential to unite the activists, human rights organizations, academics, humanitarians, and the religious community.

In November 2012, Jody Williams took a step in that direction, teaming up with Human Rights Watch and Harvard Law School's International Human Rights Clinic to release a report called 'Losing Humanity: The Case Against Killer Robots'[320] and announce the beginning of a campaign to ban the development, production, and use of fully autonomous weapons through an international legally binding instrument.

For most activists, however, banning autonomous drones would be good but not nearly enough. 'It would be a big mistake to just focus on autonomous drones,' said organizer Nick Mottern. 'Our goal should be to ban all weaponized drones. This new kind of warfare where the US and others feel they can attack anyplace, anytime, must be opposed, just as the overwhelming invasion of privacy with surveillance drones intimidating entire populations—from Waziristan to Gaza—must be stopped.'[321]

Conclusion

Over a steak dinner and a couple glasses of wine, former CIA acting general counsel John Rizzo—'a bearded, elegant 63-year-old who wears cuff links and pale yellow ties'—discussed the CIA's drone attacks with *Newsweek*'s Tara McKelvey.[322] Referring to a suspected Pakistani militant being 'blown to bits' as he got out of his car, Rizzo said he had reviewed the attack on video and concluded that it was 'very businesslike.' Rizzo said he liked to observe the killings via live footage at CIA headquarters in Virginia because he was concerned that they be done 'in the cleanest possible way.'

'Clean' is defined as minimal collateral damage, but it also has another meaning: Drone attacks are 'clean' because they are not meant to detain, or maim, or disarm, or capture. They are meant to kill, to extinguish a life—and potential public relations problems—on the spot.

'Since the US political and legal situation has made

aggressive interrogation a questionable activity anyway, there is less reason to seek to capture rather than kill,' wrote American University's law professor Kenneth Anderson. 'And if one intends to kill, the incentive is to do so from a standoff position because it removes potentially messy questions of surrender.'[323]

Think about it: Why bother with a cumbersome and extended extradition process when a Hellfire missile can handle the job, without the risk of a messy trial and perhaps even an embarrassing acquittal? While a few human rights groups might complain following an extrajudicial assassination-by-drone, unlike a prisoner at Guantánamo Bay, the dead man isn't a lingering pock on America's image abroad. Armed with that knowledge, politicians have an incentive to resort to lethal force first, usually sentencing people to death on evidence so flimsy it would never stand up in a court of law—or even a military tribunal.

The way US policymakers see it, drones are the ideal way to deal with violent extremists. Defense Secretary Leon Panetta called drone attacks the 'only game in town in terms of confronting or trying to disrupt the Al Qaeda leadership.'[324]

This mindset only seems to be getting more Orwellian, with revelations in the *Washington Post* that the Obama administration has been secretly developing a next-generation targeting list called the 'disposition matrix.' A blueprint designed to pursue terrorists for the next ten years, the matrix developed by the National Counterterrorism Center augments the separate but overlapping kill lists of the CIA and the military's Joint Special Operations Command.

President Obama institutionalized the practice of targeted killing, transforming ad hoc elements of emergency measures developed after 9/11 into a counterterrorism infrastructure designed to sustain a permanent war.

In October 2012, the CIA was reportedly pushing for an expansion of the agency's fleet of armed drones. The proposal reflected the agency's ten-year transformation from its pre-9/11 role as a spy agency into a paramilitary force. A year after Defense Secretary Leon Panetta had announced that Al Qaeda was nearly defeated, officials began talking about new threats beyond Pakistan, Yemen and Somalia. The target was now North Africa, where US officials said Al Qaeda had seized territory and smuggled weapons out of Libya after the fall of Muammar Qaddafi. Mali, Libya, Algeria, Nigeria, and even Egypt are places where US officials speculated that Al Qaeda might take root.

After ten years of war, government officials, defense contractors, and policymakers were more interested in looking for new threats—continuing the 'Whac-A-Mole' approach—than in looking for solutions.

In areas where Al Qaeda was suspected of operating, way more effort has been put into reinforcing local military structures than strengthening civilian authorities and civil society. The same for shoring up (often repressive) intelligence apparatuses instead of cultivating relationships of trust with tribal elders and other community leaders.

What happened to the old-fashioned idea of negotiations? Diplomacy? Peace talks? Reconciliation? Did they all suddenly disappear post-9/11?

I hear all the time that peace activists are naive, that it is impossible to talk to extremists—people who have no regard for the lives of innocents, people capable of strapping on suicide vests and blowing up a bunch of innocent bystanders.

But in my experiences in conflict zones the world over, there are always people to talk to. From members of Hamas in Gaza to Baathists under Saddam's Iraq to the Taliban in Afghanistan to government officials in Iran, it is a major blunder to label all our perceived enemies as extremists incapable of rational conversation. People join militant groups for many reasons—religious, family, social pressure, revenge for some wrong they experienced, political ideology, poverty. With such diversity of motives, there are always some people who can be enticed to talk about peace. Our goal should be to seek them out, to strengthen the moderates. Unfortunately, our actions have often only served to embolden the extremists.

Consider Somalia.

After nearly two decades of fighting among rival warlords, a period of unrest that itself followed decades of brutal rule by a US-backed dictator, the people of Somalia began to experience some measure of peace when in 2006 a coalition of groups called the Islamic Courts Union (ICU) took power in Mogadishu. For the first time in years, Somalia's capital was safe enough to go out at night without a heavily armed security detail.

But there was a problem: that word 'Islamic.' Despite the ICU representing a moderate strain of Islam, the Bush administration was convinced that the ICU was a dangerous terrorist organization that, if left in power, would give groups like Al Qaeda sanctuary. Since US troops were bogged down in Iraq and Afghanistan, the Bush administration outsourced the job, backing Ethiopia with money for a proxy invasion and backing up the Ethiopian troops with aerial attacks, including drones.

They pushed the ICU out of power—and pushed Somalia back into chaos. The moderate ICU splintered into a number of now-radicalized groups like Al Shabab, the emergence of which was then used to justify ever more US intervention in Somalia in the form of stepped-up air strikes.

Al Shabab has been most active in precisely those parts of Somalia where the US and its cohorts—first Ethiopia and then Kenya—have been most active. 'Somalia is an example of the US military policy gone completely amok,' said Emira Woods, director of Foreign Policy in Focus. 'It helped destabilize Somalia and strengthen Al Shabab, which barely existed before the US heavy-handed response to the ICU.'

In Iraq and Afghanistan, years of war with high-tech drones did not lead to victories. Regarding drone strikes in Pakistan, counterinsurgency expert David Kilcullen and former Army officer Andrew McDonald Exum wrote in a 2009 opinion piece: 'Every one of these dead noncombatants represents an alienated family, a new desire for revenge, and more recruits for a militant movement that has grown exponentially even as the drone strikes have increased.[325] They concluded that it would be in the best interest of the American and Pakistani people to declare a moratorium on drone strikes in Pakistan.

New York Times reporter David Rohde, emerging from seven months as a Taliban hostage in Afghanistan and Pakistan, wrote that his kidnappers' hatred for the United States was fueled in part by civilians being killed by drones.[326] 'To my captors,' he wrote, 'they were proof that the United States was a hypocritical and duplicitous power that flouted international law.'

Pashtun tribal culture considers face-to-face combat honorable. Firing a missile at faceless people from a bunker thousands of miles away? Not so much. And someone in tribal society who has lost his family members in a drone strike is bound by the Pashtun honor code—*Pashtunwali*—to retaliate and opt for *badal* (revenge or justice).

Opposition to drone strikes is not just in the tribal areas, but all over Pakistan. A June 2012 Pew opinion poll found an astonishing result: three in four Pakistanis (74 per cent) considered the US an enemy.[327] When Foreign Minister Hina Rabbani Khar was asked why there was so much animosity towards the United States, she gave a one word answer: drones.

Suspending drone strikes won't stop Islamic radicals altogether, but continuing the unmanned killing only exacerbates the problem. That's because while violent extremists may be unpopular, for a frightened population they may seem less of a threat than an omnipresent, hovering enemy that at any moment could choose to eliminate one's loved ones with a Hellfire missile. Extremists—Al Qaeda, the Taliban, Al Shabab—capitalize on that fear, casting themselves as the defenders of the people, while at the same time callously killing innocent people, local police, and armed forces, and destroying schools and infrastructure.

The brutal shooting of fifteen-year-old Pakistani Malala Yousafzai in October 2012 exposed the Taliban's twisted mindset. The shooting backfired, igniting a global outpouring of support for this courageous young advocate of educating girls, leading to a UN declaration of 'Malala Day' on November 10, 2012, and promises of more funding for schools.

More important, though, was the well of disgust that arose within Pakistan and the determination to make sure the Taliban did not succeed. Pakistanis organized rallies throughout the country; girls everywhere, even in Swat Valley where Malala was shot, expressed their determination to return to school; fathers vowed to protect the schools themselves; and citizens delivered one million signatures to the government demanding free and compulsory education. Malala's shooting awoke Pakistan's silent majority who stood up and said 'Enough' to the Taliban's threats and oppression.

At the same time, this worldwide focus on Malala forced the government to undertake a nationwide search for her aggressors. While this is just one case out of so many, the spotlight helped set an example of Pakistani police and military action, civil society activism, and global support as the way forward.

Ultimately, this is precisely how extremism will be defeated. Drone strikes make that task harder, not easier, by driving those victimized by anonymous terror-from-the-sky into the arms of terrorists.

Even if one concedes the morality of killing out-and-out terrorists without trials, that's not what is really at issue. Sure, drones do kill bad people who might deserve their fate, but they also kill a lot of innocents—usually at the same time. So the question is not just whether it's morally right to execute killers, but whether it's right to do so even if that means killing innocent men, women and children—and whether, in the end, doing so really makes us all any safer.

Air strikes have not only blown up perceived enemies and innocent people, but also peace talks. In November 2011, a US air strike meant to target the Taliban in Pakistan mistakenly killed Pakistani soldiers who were camped along the Afghan border, leaving two dozen dead. The strike came just before a long-planned major diplomatic gathering on Bonn, Germany, where over one hundred countries and international organizations were gathering to discuss how to end the war in Afghanistan. Pakistan was a key player in the discussions.

But in the wake of the air strike and public outrage, the Pakistani government refused to attend the gathering, destroying the long-awaited attempt at peace negotiations. An anonymous State Department official complained to the *Washington Post* that this was one more example of the disconnect between the military's short-term security objectives and the State Department's long-term diplomatic goals.[328] 'In a lot of ways, diplomacy is this historical anachronism,' the official lamented.

At the Aspen Security Forum marking ten years since 9/11, retired admiral and former Director of National Intelligence Dennis Blair, who was pushed out of the Obama administration in 2010, questioned the drone attacks and the entire focus on terrorism from both a strategic and economic perspective. He called it a 'global game of Whac-A-Mole—something to keep you busy,' but not a strategy because it alienated the very people whose cooperation was needed to overcome terrorism in the long term. Blair estimated there were 4,000 Al Qaeda members around the globe. With most of the yearly intelligence budget of $80 billion devoted to catching them, that comes to $20 million per terrorist per year. 'You think — wow, $20 million. Is that proportionate?' he asked.

Blair said that in the decade since 9/11, less than twenty Americans had been killed on US soil by terrorists (fourteen of them in the Ft. Hood massacre when a Muslim soldier went berserk after the army refused to discharge him). He contrasted the terror body count with deaths from car accidents and street crime, which killed more than one million Americans in the same time frame. 'What is it that justifies this amount of money on this narrow problem versus the other ways we have to protect American lives?' asked Blair. 'I think that's the question we have to think ourselves through here at the tenth year anniversary.'

Retired Lieutenant Colonel William Astore wondered the same thing. Looking back at the 'shoe bomber' and the 'underwear bomber,' he asked, 'Why did the criminally inept actions of those two losers garner so much attention in the media?' As the most powerful nation on earth, we should have 'shared a collective belly laugh at the absurdity and incompetence of those "attacks" and gone about our business.' Instead, he said, they were used as yet another excuse to feed the 'web of crony corporations, lobbyists, politicians and retired military types who pass through Washington's revolving door...engorged by untold trillions devoted to a national security and intelligence complex that dominates Washington.'[329]

Indeed, since 9/11, the Pentagon and CIA have been lavished with funding, especially for their drone programs. Even during the post-recession budget crisis, the funding for drone research and acquisition increased. When Secretary of Defense Leon Panetta talked about 2013 budget cuts, including cuts in troop numbers, weapons systems, and military benefits, he made it clear that 'unmanned systems' would be given priority.

In contrast, the State Department has been reeling from budget cuts. One of the only areas of its budget that hasn't been slashed is funding for its operations for Iraq, where the State Department—after the December 2011 pull-out of the US military—is now responsible for such 'diplomatic activities' as overseeing thousands of armed guards, training the Iraqi police, and operating a fleet of drones.

In Pakistan, the State Department is forced to collaborate on drone killings with the CIA. US Ambassador Cameron Munter was put in the most undiplomatic position of having to give a thumbs up or thumbs down on each of these strikes. He reportedly criticized the CIA's strikes for driving American policy, complaining to a colleague that 'he didn't realize his main job was to kill people.'[330]

'Can you imagine if the Pakistani ambassador to Washington DC Sherry Rehman was required to say yea or nay to killing people in Texas every other day?' asked Reprieve lawyer Clive Stafford Smith. 'She would be assassinated if she wasn't prosecuted for the death penalty in Texas itself. What they are doing is making the State Department's job absolutely impossible.'

In the past decade, the State Department has become a weaker and weaker institution, watching its anemic attempts at diplomacy go up in smoke. It's only gotten worse since Predators and Reapers became key players in US foreign policy. With drones as the new workhorse, diplomacy—the forgotten art of talking to one another—has been unceremoniously taken out to pasture.

'Forty years ago American universities used to teach the art of diplomacy, now they teach about national security and strategic studies—all militarized ways of thinking about international issues,' lamented former diplomat and retired US Army Colonel Ann Wright. 'Consider the belligerent policies of the State Department during the tenures of the last secretaries of state: Madeline Albright, Colin Powell, Condoleezza Rice and Hillary Clinton. They were not diplomats representing nonviolent resolutions to international challenges, but instead were extensions of the Defense Department carrying out the military policy of the United States for the president they served.'

Yet, when we look at the forty-year history of groups

once designated as terrorist, a RAND study shows that the primary factor for their demise was not military defeat but negotiations. Of 268 terrorist groups, 43 percent ended through participation in the political process, 40 percent through effective policing, and a mere 7 percent through military force.[331]

In the US struggle against terrorism that has been so biased toward a military response, we not only have a dire need to create more diplomacy, we also have a dire need for more citizen involvement. In the United States, foreign policy has only on the rarest of occasions been subject to democratic input, and typically only when body bags containing American soldiers dominated the evening news. With drones, the president can choose to take the nation to war with no Americans putting their bodies on the line. In a more perfect world, this would not have an impact on decisions to use lethal force; the justness of a war, after all, does not hinge on whether one's own side of a conflict might suffer casualties.

On the globe we actually live in, though, nationalism and a bias toward the familiar tends to lead people to feel more for their compatriots than for the nameless, faceless 'Other.'

And with US wars today, the Other is not only nameless and faceless, but invisible. Have you ever seen a drone victim on the news? Have you seen pictures of body parts hanging from trees, houses turned to rubble, mothers wailing in grief? The mainstream media, after cheerleading for war and enthusiastically covering the initial shock-and-awe volley of missiles, quickly became bored with

America's imperial exploits. And with the rise of drone warfare that poses no risk to Americans, they aren't about to spend time covering blown-up foreigners, especially when there's something important like a celebrity breakup to report.

Imagine if the tables were turned, though. Imagine if Cuba was operating drones in southern Florida, surveilling Cuban-Americans and executing confessed terrorists like Luis Posada Carriles. What if the Chinese were pursuing Tibetan separatists around the globe with drones, or Russia was doing the same thing to Chechens whom it considered terrorists?

Pretty soon one might not need to imagine. Other countries are sure to follow the precedent set by the United States government, the one that says it's acceptable to bypass the formality of the law and simply assassinate another country's citizens—or your own—so long as some anonymous official whispers the word 'terrorist' in a journalist's ear. Israel is already doing the same thing. China, Russia, Iran—indeed, the rest of the world—are watching.

Instead of the rigorous public debate one would expect from a democratic society faced with these complex ethical questions regarding remote-controlled killing, the mainstream media is silent, most religious leaders are silent, as are most elected officials. And the anti-war movement, so vocal and vibrant during the Bush years, lost its voice when Barack Obama became president.

That provided the space for President Obama to continue his predecessor's wars and rain ever more

Hellfire missiles overseas with less public debate than if he were a sports executive proposing to trade a first round draft pick. Sure, there have been wars with much greater casualty counts. But no president has ever carried out so many secret, targeted killings. Even former president Jimmy Carter was appalled at the killing of an untold number of civilians in drone attacks, with each attack approved by the highest authorities in Washington. 'This would have been unthinkable in previous times,' Carter said.[332]

It's quite astounding that the Obama administration has killed thousands of suspected militants and civilians alike, including US citizens, in undeclared, illegal wars with nary a whisper of 'impeachment' on Capitol Hill.

Even if they were so inclined, it's not clear lawmakers would be able to dig up much about the wars being remotely waged in their names. Between the CIA, private contractors and the Pentagon's ultra-secretive Joint Special Operations Command, the Obama administration has been able to wage undeclared wars in ways that shield it from public scrutiny. The convergence of military and intelligence resources has created blind spots in Congressional oversight, as the CIA briefs intelligence committees and JSOC reports to armed services committees. Since the briefs are secret, the committees can't compare notes to gain a comprehensive understanding. And it's only the relevant committees—and sometimes only the committee heads—that get briefed, leaving most officials in the dark.

But don't assume the lawmakers are clamoring to learn more. When there's a Democrat in the White House, other Democrats in positions of authority—even the ostensibly anti-war ones—have shown no real inclination to investigate their own president's wars of choice, particularly when there's no real risk to the Americans piloting the drones. And Republicans, being the less subtle pro-war party in Washington, are generally in favor of bombing everywhere and would rather investigate community groups like ACORN than something as banal as an illegal, only winkingly-acknowledged war.

There is one voice talking about drones in Congress, though. It's the self-described 'industry's voice on Capitol Hill'—the Congressional Unmanned Systems Caucus. This group of fifty lawmakers, who as of 2012 represented about one in eight members of the House of Representatives and just under half of the defense appropriations subcommittee, helps make sure that even killer drones enjoy a voice in Washington.

It seems that, like corporations, robots are people too.

A membership map provided by the caucus shows that its bipartisan membership spans the range of acceptable opinion in the US capital, from Republican hawk to militarist Democrat. From California conservative Buck McKeon to California liberal Linda Sánchez, the members demonstrate the drone industry's broad geographic and political support.

The group's mission statement says the members recognize 'the urgent need to rapidly develop and deploy more Unmanned Systems in support of ongoing civil, military, and law enforcement operations.' These congresspeople, many of whom are fiscal conservatives busy slashing social programs in the name of the taxpayer, also pledge to support 'policies and budgets that promote a large, more robust national security unmanned system capability.'

Contrary to some of its more strident critics, the United States does indeed have a functioning representative democracy. It's just that those being represented aren't the same 'we the people' that they teach in grade school.

Peter Singer, author of *Wired For War*, says that we're at the Wright Brothers Flier stage of unmanned aircraft and that debating drones is like debating the merits of computers in 1979: 'They are here to stay, and the boom has barely begun.'[333]

But we are constantly having vigorous debates about computers. In January 2012, for example, when Congress attempted to pass a law that would have shut down Internet sites accused of violating copyright laws, they were flooded with so many millions of calls and petitions that they had to table the legislation.

We need the same vigorous debate and activism around a technology like drones that has such a profound impact on our reputation, the ethical foundations of our society, the lives of innocent people, and ultimately, our security as a nation.

We need to re-examine who we are as a nation—and who we want to be. Do we want to be a country where people press a kill button by day and then rush home for dinner with the family? Do we want our president making decisions about who will be on this week's kill list? Do we want to accept a 'disposition matrix' that will keep us at war for at least the next decade? Do we want the best minds of our country—and our scarce tax dollars—to focus on ever more ominous machines to kill and spy?

With the US military now using thousands of drones and FAA opening domestic skies to drones, the conversation is long overdue.

Not all uses of unmanned aircraft are bad. Drones were used after the earthquake in Japan to observe radiation levels at the Fukushima nuclear plant. They were used in Australia to inspect the state of wildlife after a massive flood. They have great potential to help firefighters by hovering over swaths of burning forests.

Environmental, human rights and even protest groups are starting to use drones. The Sea Shepherd Conservation Society is launching small drones over the vast expanse of ocean to spot illegal whaling. Human rights groups are advocating that drones be used to spy on regimes cracking down on their people, as in the case of Syria.[334] Protest groups in Poland have flown drones over the heads of police to monitor their conduct, a tactic that Occupy Wall Street in New York mimicked with $300 toy mini-drones sold in Brookstone.

But what is fueling the drone boom is neither scientific missions nor creative activists, but state-sponsored assassinations and semi-covert wars. And unfortunately it is those latter pursuits—not a cure for cancer, say, or replacement for fossil fuels—to which some of the best scientific minds in the world today are dedicating their time.

Drones now under development in research centers all over the country are designed to be more lethal, have greater autonomy, stay airborne for longer periods and have a more precise, broader vision of the battlefield. One technology under development is termed the 'swarm.' Like a swarm of angry bees, a bevy of unmanned aerial, ground and sea vehicles would autonomously converge on enemy troops, aircraft and ships. Then they'd jointly decide their plan of attack, engage the enemy—and beat the hell out of 'em, of course—all without direct human intervention.

Drone surveillance will become more all-encompassing. The US Air Force description of current drone projects says new 'unmanned aircraft systems (Vulture) and airships (ISIS) can remain aloft for years...large airships containing football-field-size radars give extreme resolution/persistence.' One can imagine whole swaths of nations or whole nations subjected to a kind of 'dronesphere' in which all public activity is monitored without respect for national borders or personal privacy in a way far beyond what has ever been technologically possible.

Of course, these new systems are not just for use overseas. The surveillance capabilities of drones and their increasing use by domestic law enforcement agencies in the United States and elsewhere threaten to eviscerate what's left of our privacy rights. The sensors on drones are designed to monitor miles of terrain. No matter how targeted an investigation, you always risk the prying eye of the state observing your affairs. Who needs to live in a glass house when the government, armed with drones and million-dollar heat sensors, can already see whatever it wants?

Drones aren't a unique evil—but that's just the point. Drones don't revolutionize surveillance; they are a progressive evolution in making spying, at home and abroad, more pervasive. Drones don't revolutionize warfare; they are, rather, a progressive evolution in making murder clean and easy. That's why the increased reliance on drones for killing and spying is not to be praised, but refuted. And challenged.

The burden is now squarely on we the people to reassert our rights and push back against the normalization of drones as a military and law enforcement tool. The use of drones needs to be limited, transparent and, at the least, acknowledged; it's no less a war if the plane firing the missile is remotely operated. Our ability to curb the use of UAVs—rescuing hurricane victims, yes, carrying out extrajudicial killings, no—will not only determine the future of warfare and individual privacy, but shape our character as a nation and how we live together as a global human community.

Acknowledgments

First, let me thank Charles Davis for his wonderful writing and research help; Allison McCracken for being such a terrific assistant; Rafia Zakaria for her work on the victims in Pakistan; Nadira Sheralam for her careful editing; Kindra Wyatt for her painstaking documentation; and Nancy Mancias for her research and action guide.

I also want to give a shout out to my CODEPINK sisters on the national team, who make this work so rewarding: codirectors Jodie Evans and Rae Abileah, Joan Stallard, Sasha Gelzin, Farida Sheralam, Janet Weil, Nancy Kricorian, Melanie Butler, Kristin Ess Schurr, Gayle Brandeis, and Lisa Savage, and my Global Exchange colleagues, especially Kirsten Moller.

My opposition to drone warfare has deepened by witnessing the commitment of the unsung activists around the country who have been protesting at Air Force bases and dronemaker offices for years. These include Kathy Kelly, Nick Mottern, Brian Terrell, Jim Haber, Ann Wright, Ray McGovern, Ed Kinane, Mary Anne Grady, Judy Bello, Vicki Ross, Debra Sweet, Father Louis Vitale, Father Jerry Zawada, the Catholic Workers, the Creech 14 and Hancock 38, World Can't Wait, and the War Resisters.

I am inspired by my CODEPINK sisters who speak out so passionately on behalf of drone victims they have never met. Many thanks to Toby Blome for her pioneering work, as well as Nancy Mancias, Martha Hubert, Leslie Angeline, Eleanor Levine, Liz Hourican, Cynthia Papermaster, Marie Bravo, Zanne Joi, Chris Nelson, Caroline Kittrell, Shirley and Pamela Osgood, Zohreh Whitaker, Beverly McGain, Susan Witka, Renay Davis, and Dianne Budd. I extend special gratitude to Candace Ross, the Goddess Temple priestess, for her extraordinary hosting of protesters at the Guest House near Creech Air Force Base. I also want to recognize Jean Aguerre for her steadfast and effective Not 1 More Acre Campaign.

I received valuable input from many colleagues, including Pratap Chaterjee, Clive Stafford Smith, Jody Williams, Peter Ansaro, Noel Sharkey, Mark Gubrud, Fran Quigley, Tom Barry and Polly Miller, as well as interns Rosie Platzer and Viannka Lopez. Special thanks to Tara Murray at Reprieve and Mizra Shahzad Akbar for his work with drone victims in Pakistan, Chris Cole of Drone Wars UK and the great UK activists whom I look forward to working with.

It was due to a chance meeting with OR Books publisher John Oakes that I had the opportunity to write this book, and I thank him and the wonderful crew at OR for their encouragement.

Finally, I owe a debt of gratitude to my partner Tighe Barry for always being so thoughtful and supportive, and to my children Arlen and Maya for motivating me to leave a better world for them.

Further Resources

BOOKS/REPORTS

Philip Alston, 'Report of the Special Rapporteur on Extrajudicial, Summary or Arbitrary Executions,' United Nations General Assembly, Human Rights Council, Fourteenth Session, May 23, 2010.

Chris Cole, *Convenient Killing: Armed Drones and the 'Playstation' Mentality*. Oxford: The Fellowship of Reconciliation, 2010.

Matt J. Martin and Charles W. Sasser, *Predator: The Remote-control Air War over Iraq and Afghanistan: A Pilot's Story*. Minneapolis, MN: Zenith, 2010.

Mary Ellen O'Connell, 'Lawful Use of Combat Drones—Hearing: Rise of the Drones II: Examining the Legality of Unmanned Targeting,' Subcommittee on National Security and Foreign Affairs, US Congress, April 28, 2010.

Chris Rogers, 'CIVIC: Campaign for Innocent Victims in Conflict—REPORT: Pakistan 2010.' CIVIC: Campaign for Innocent Victims in Conflict.

P. W. Singer, *Wired for War: The Robotics Revolution and Conflict in the Twenty-first Century*. New York: Penguin, 2009.

The Civilian Impact of Drones: Unexamined Costs, Unanswered Questions, Center for Civilians in Conflict and Human Rights Clinic at Columbia Law School, September 29, 2012.

Congressional Budget Office, 'Policy Options for Unmanned Aircraft Systems,' Publication 4083, Washington, DC, June 2011.

Living Under Drones: Death, Injury, and Trauma to Civilians from US Drone Practices in Pakistan, International Human Rights and Conflict Resolution Clinic of Stanford Law School and Global Justice Clinic of NYU School of Law, October 2012.

United Kingdom Ministry of Defence, 'The UK Approach to Unmanned Aircraft Systems,' Joint Doctrine, 2011.

'Does Unmanned Make Unacceptable? Exploring the Debate on using Drones and Robots in Warfare,' IKV Pax Christi, May 2011.

ORGANIZATIONS

American Civil Liberties Union: www.aclu.org

Amnesty International: www.amnesty.org

Bureau of Investigative Journalism: www.thebureau investigates.com

Campaign for Innocent Victims in Conflict (CIVIC): www. civicworldwide.org

Catholic Worker Movement: www.catholicworker.org

Center for Constitutional Rights: ccrjustice.org

CODEPINK: www.codepink.org

Drone Campaign Network: www.dronecampaignnetwork. org.uk

Drone Wars UK: dronewarsuk.wordpress.com

Fellowship of Reconciliation, England: www.for.org.uk

Global Network Against Weapons and Nuclear Power in Space: www.space4peace.org

Human Rights Watch: www.hrw.org

International Committee for Robot Arms Control: www. icrac.co/uk

Know Drones: www.knowdrones.org

Nevada County Peace Center: www.ncpeace.org

Nuclear Resister: www.nuclearresister.org

Reprieve: www.reprieve.org.uk

The Nevada Desert Experience: www.nevadadesert experience.org

United Against the Drones: Unitedagainstthedrones. wordpress.com

Upstate NY Coalition to End the Drones: upstatedroneaction.org

Veterans For Peace: veteransforpeace.org

Voices for Creative Nonviolence: vcnv.org

Women in Black: www.womeninblack.org

World Can't Wait: www.worldcantwait.net

WEBSITES

Antiwar.com

wired.com/dangerroom, especially Noah Shachtman and Spencer Ackerman

Association for Unmanned Vehicle Systems International (AUVSI), www.auvsi.org

No Drones Network, nodronesnetwork.blogspot.com

Know Drones, knowdrones.com

Drones Watch, droneswatch.org

Lobbying Spending Database, OpenSecrets.org

Smithsonian Air and Space Museum drone exhibit: www. nasm.si.edu/exhibitions/gal104/uav.cfm

Congressional Unmanned Systems Caucus: unmannedsystemscaucus.mckeon.house.gov

TomDispatch.com, especially Nick Turse and Tom Engelhardt

FILMS/VIDEOS

Remote Control War, available on DVD and Netflix: www.amazon.com/Remote-Control-Narrated-Anne-Marie-MacDonald/dp/B004RV70JW

'America's use for domestic drones' Al Jazeera English, Dec 7, 2011, www.youtube.com/watch?v=QTLtNgSRXyc

'The Real Casualties of the Drone War,' RT TV, December 14, 2011, www.youtube.com/watch?v=x0aw4ym6l6c

Robot Wars, *Faultlines*, Al Jazeera, www.youtube.com/watch?v=TyJoJUs14bc

CODEPINK at the AUVSI press conference, www.youtube.com/watch?v=wOcF6g2YlcQ

Stop the Arms Fair 2011—UK Anti Drones Action: www.youtube.com/watch?v=n8NaCgAl27o

With song: www.youtube.com/watch?v=DQF0XOMqcDc

Endnotes

1 Carl Conetta, 'Operation Enduring Freedom: Why a Higher Rate of Civilian Bombing Casualties,' Project on Defense Alternatives. Commonwealth Institute of Cambridge, MA, USA. N.p., n.d.

2 P. W. Singer, *Wired for War: Robotics Revolution and Conflict in the Twenty-first Century*, Penguin Press, 2009, p. 61.

3 Christopher Rogers, 'Civilians in Armed Conflict: Civilian Harm and Conflict in Northwest Pakistan,' CIVIC, 2010, p. 20.

4 Jo Becker and Scott Shane, 'Secret "Kill List" Proves a Test of Obama's Principles and Will,' *The New York Times*, May 29, 2012.

5 Scott Wilson and Jon Cohen, 'Poll Finds Broad Support for Obama's Counterterrorism Policies,' *The Washington Post*, February 8, 2012.

6 Pew Research Center, 'Global Opinion of Obama Slips, International Policies Faulted,' June 13, 2012.

7 Khawar Rizvi, Personal interview by author, Washington, D.C., May 3, 2010.

8 'Politics is Funny,' *A Tiny Revolution*, May 2, 2010.

9 Rod Powers, 'Military Word/Phrase Origins,' United States Military Information.

10 Jeremiah Gertler, 'U.S. Unmanned Aerial Systems,' p. 1, *Congressional Research Service.*

11 Peter Finn, 'Rise of the Drone: From Calif. Garage to Multibillion-dollar Defense industry,' *The Washington Post*, December 24, 2011.

12 Chris Cole, 'Convenient Killing: Armed Drones and the "Playstation" Mentality,' The Fellowship of Reconciliation, England, 2010.

13 Elizabeth Bone, 'Unmanned Aerial Vehicles: Background and Issues for Congress,' *Congressional Research Service*, April 25, 2003.

14 Nic Robertson, 'How Robot Drones Revolutionized the Face of Warfare,' CNN, July 23, 2009.
15 Jeremiah Gertler, 'U.S. Unmanned Aerial Systems,' Summary, *Congressional Research Service*, January 3, 2012.
16 'Program Acquisition Costs by Weapon System,' Office of the Under Secretary of Defense, February 2011 p. 1-1.
17 'General Atomics MQ-9 Reaper,' Wikipedia.
18 Jeremiah Gertler, 'U.S. Unmanned Aerial Systems,' *Congressional Research Service*, January 3, 2012 p. 22.
19 David S. Cloud, 'Contractors' Role Grows in Drone Missions, Worrying Some in the Military,' McClatchy News, December 29, 2011.
20 Elisabeth Bumiller and Thom Shanker, 'Microdrones, Some as Small as Bugs, Are Poised to Alter War,' *The New York Times*, June 20, 2011.
21 Ibid.
22 David S. Cloud, 'Contractors' Role Grows in Drone Missions, Worrying Some in the Military,' McClatchy News, December 29, 2011.
23 'Policy Options for Unmanned Aircraft Systems,' Publication 4083, Congressional Budget Office, Washington DC, June 2011 p. 31.
24 Ibid.
25 Christopher Drew, 'Drones Are U.S. Weapons of Choice in Fighting Qaeda,' *The New York Times*, March 16, 2009.
26 Associated Press, 'U.S. Deploys Drones Against Somali Pirates,' CBS News, October 24, 2009.
27 David Zucchino, 'Military Drone Aircraft: Losses in Afghanistan, Iraq,' *The Los Angeles Times*, July 6, 2010.
28 Brian Bennett, 'Military Global Hawk Drone Crashes in Maryland,' *The Los Angeles Times*, June 11, 2012.
29 'Oops! Keystroke Goof Sets Navy Drone to Self-Destruct,' Fox News, July 19, 2011.
30 Joshua Stewart, 'Fire Scout Report Outlines Tech Glitches,' *Navy Times*, July 2011.
31 Noah Shachtman, 'Insurgents Intercept Drone Video in King-size Security Breach,' Wired.com, December 17, 2009.
32 Noah Shachtman, 'Exclusive: Computer Virus Hits U.S. Drone Fleet,' Wired.com, October 7, 2011.
33 Nic Robertson, 'How Robot Drones Revolutionized the Face of Warfare,' CNN.com International, July 23, 2009.
34 Chris Woods and Christina Lamb, 'Obama Terror Drones: CIA Tactics in Pakistan Include Targeting Rescuers and Funerals,' Bureau of Investigative Journalism, February 4, 2012.
35 Jane Mayer, 'The Risks of the C.I.A.'s Predator Drones,' *The New Yorker*, October 26, 2009.
36 'UK Faults Self and US for Plane Shootdown,' *Space War*, May 14, 2004.
37 David Zucchino and David S. Cloud, 'U.S. Deaths in Drone Strike Due to Miscommunication, Report Says,' *The Los Angeles Times*, October 14, 2011.

38 Medea Benjamin, 'Did You Hear the Joke About the Predator Drone That Bombed?' Common Dreams, May 5, 2010.
39 Elisabeth Bumiller and Thom Shanker, 'Microdrones, Some as Small as Bugs, Are Poised to Alter War,' *The New York Times*, June 20, 2011.
40 '2010 Top 100 Contractors: General Atomics,' *Washington Technology*, Eagle Eye Publisher.
41 W.J. Hennigan, 'General Atomics: Drones Create a Buzz in Southern California Aerospace Industry,' *The Los Angeles Times*, September 11, 2010.
42 Greg Miller, 'CIA Seeks to Expand Drone Fleet, Officials Say,' *The Washington Post*, October 18, 2012.
43 Zach Rosenburg, 'US Air Force Orders General Atomics Avenger,' *Aviation and Aerospace News*, Flightglobal.com, December 12, 2011.
44 Jen Dimascio, 'New Drones Net Rosy Skies for Makers,' Politico.com, November 23, 2009.
45 Steve Henn and Robert Brodsky, '"Top Gun"' of Travel,' *iWatch News*, June 5, 2006.
46 Gopal Ratnam, 'General Atomics Wins Approval to Sell First Predator Drones in Middle East,' Bloomberg, July 20, 2010.
47 'Lobbying Spending Database: General Atomics,' *OpenSecrets*, 2011.
48 Scott Shane, 'Coming Soon: The Drone Arms Race,' *The New York Times*, October 9, 2011.
49 'AeroVironment Receives $16 Million Order for Raven Unmanned Aircraft Systems Contractor Logistics Support,' *Business Wire*, September 8, 2011.
50 'AeroVironment Receives $7.3 Million Order for Puma Unmanned Aircraft System Support Services,' *Business Wire*, October 20, 2011.
51 David Wichner, 'Distributed Common Ground System,' Raytheon Company.
52 David Wichner, 'Raytheon's New Griffin Fit for Drone,' *Arizona Daily Star*, August 22, 2010.
53 David Wichner, 'Raytheon Developing Drone-fired Weapon,' *StarNet*, April 25, 2011.
54 Spencer Ackerman, 'Mini-Missile Promises to Shrink the Drone War,' Wired.com, December 1, 2011.
55 Rikki Mitchell, 'Drones That Stay Airborne Forever,' *StarNet*, February 27, 2011.
56 W.J. Hennigan, 'Phantom Ray Test Flight: Boeing's Robotic Jet Phantom Ray Takes Maiden Test Flight,' *The Los Angeles Times*, May 4, 2011.
57 Brian Wingfield, 'Drone Wars,' Forbes.com, June 1, 2009.
58 1st Lt. Jason Sweeney, 'Armed and Dangerous: The Gray Eagle Goes Lethal,' General Atomics, April 9, 2011.
59 'Factsheets: RQ-4 Global Hawk,' Official website of the US Air Force.
60 Christopher Drew, 'Costly Drone Is Poised to Replace U-2 Spy Plane,' *The New York Times*, August 3, 2011.

61 Steve Zaloga and David Rockwell, 'UAV Market Set for 10 Years of Growth,' *EIJ - Earth Imaging Journal*.
62 Christopher Drew, 'Costly Drone Is Poised to Replace U-2 Spy Plane,' *The New York Times*, August 3, 2011.
63 W.J. Hennigan, 'U.S. May Rely on Aging U-2 Spy Planes Longer Than Expected,' *The Los Angeles Times*, January 28, 2012.
64 'Lobbying Spending Database: General Atomics, 2011,' OpenSecrets.org.
65 'Lockheed Martin Announces Fourth Quarter 2010 Results,' LockheedMartin.com.
66 'Lobbying Spending Database,' OpenSecrets.org.
67 'Lockheed Martin,' Wikipedia.
68 'HELLFIRE II Missile,' LockheedMartin.com.
69 'US to Deploy Deadlier "Hellfire Romeo" Precision-strike Missiles in War against Terrorism,' Yahoo! India News, October 16, 2011.
70 Amir Khan, 'Lockheed Martin Tests Tiny Samarai UAV,' *Popular Mechanics*, August 18, 2011.
71 Stephen Trimble, 'REPORT: RQ-170 Spied Over Osama bin Laden's Bed Last Night,' *The DEW Line*, May 2011.
72 Interview with Mark Gubrud, February 3, 2012.
73 'U.S. Military Drones That Are So Small They Even Look Like Insects,' *Daily Mail Reporter*, July 12, 2011.
74 'AFRL's New Lab Focused on Micro Air Vehicles,' *AviationDayton*, May 27, 2010.
75 'U.S. Military Drones That Are So Small They Even Look Like Insects,' *Daily Mail Reporter*, July 12, 2011.
76 'Our Work,' Defense Advanced Research Projects Agency.
77 Tina Casey, 'DARPA Looks to the Crowd to Build Miniature Drones,' *TPM Idea Lab*, October 2011.
78 Alfred McCoy, 'Super Weapons and Global Dominion,' *TomDispatch*, November 9, 2012.
79 Eric Hagerman, 'Coming Soon: An Unblinking "Gorgon Stare" For Air Force Drones,' *Popular Science*, August 2009.
80 David Axe and Noah Shachtman, 'Air Force's "All-Seeing Eye" Flops Vision Test,' Wired.com, January 2011.
81 Steve Zaloga and David Rockwell, 'UAV Market Set for 10 Years of Growth,' *EIJ - Earth Imaging Journal*, 2011.
82 Charles Levinson, 'Israeli Robots Remake Battlefield,' *The Wall Street Journal*, January 13, 2010.
83 Yaakov Katz, 'Israel's Eye in the Sky,' *The Jerusalem Post*, October 17, 2011.
84 'Israel and the Rise of Drone Warfare,' *Neged Neshek*.
85 BBC World News, 'Russia "Will Buy Israeli Drones,"' BBC News, April 10, 2009.
86 Reuters, 'Russia in Talks to Buy Israeli-made Spy Drones for $100m,' *Haaretz Israeli News*, July 12, 2009.

87 'IAI Delivers 12 UAVs to Russia in Key Deal,' SpaceDaily.com, January 17, 2011.
88 AFP and Dawn.com, 'Israel is Leader in Drone Exports,' CN Publications, July 2, 2010.
89 Rajat Pandit, 'India Lines Up Israeli Drones in Race with Pak,' *The Times of India*, March 26, 2010.
90 'Say Hello to Pakistan's First Domestically Produced Armed Drone: The Burraq UCAV,' TechLahore, December 4, 2011.
91 Jeremy Page, 'China's Drones Raise Eyebrows at Air Show,' *The Wall Street Journal*, November 18, 2010.
92 Nathan Hodge, 'U.S. Military Confirms It Shot Down Iranian Drone,' Wired.com, March 16, 2009.
93 P.W. Singer, 'Will Foreign Drones One Day Attack the U.S.?,' *The Daily Beast*, February 25, 2010.
94 W.J. Hennigan, David S. Cloud, and Ken Dilanian, 'Drone that Crashed in Iran May Give Away U.S. Secrets,' *The Los Angeles Times*, December 6, 2011.
95 Brad Knickerbocker, 'US Considered Missions to Destroy RQ-170 Sentinel Drone Lost in Iran,' *The Christian Science Monitor*, December 7, 2011.
96 Patrick McGroarty, 'Two South African Defense Firms Take Aim at Niche Aircraft Market,' *The Wall Street Journal*, September 27, 2011.
97 'Colombia Makes Incursions in Developing Drones,' *Prensa Latina*, October 25, 2012.
98 Saeed Shah and Peter Beaumont, 'US Drone Strikes in Pakistan Claiming Many Civilian Victims, Says Campaigner,' *The Guardian*, July 17, 2011.
99 'Iraqi Drones Not For WMD,' CBS News, February 11, 2009.
100 Tom Vanden Brook, 'Drones Reshaping Iraq's Battlefields,' *USA Today*, July 6, 2006.
101 Associated Press, 'Use of Unmanned Drones Soars in Iraq,' MSNBC, January 1, 2008.
102 Christopher Drew, 'Drones Are Playing a Growing Role in Afghanistan,' *The New York Times*, February 19, 2010.
103 Gordon Lubold, 'As Drones Multiply in Iraq and Afghanistan, So Do Their Uses,' *The Christian Science Monitor*, March 2, 2010.
104 Ibid.
105 Tom Vanden Brook, 'Drone Attacks Hit High in Iraq,' *USA Today*, April 29, 2008.
106 Eric Schmitt and Michale S. Schmidt, 'Iraq is Angered by U.S. Drones Patrolling Its Skies,' *The New York Times*, January 29, 2012.
107 Nick Turse, 'America's Secret Empire of Drone Bases,' *The Nation*, October 17, 2011.
108 Greg Miller, 'Under Obama, an Emerging Global Apparatus for Drone Killing,' *The Washington Post*, December 27, 2011.

109 Lolita C. Baldor, 'Panetta Spills a Little on Secret CIA Drones,' Yahoo! News, October 7, 2011.

110 Daniel Benjamin and Steven Simon, *The Age of Sacred Terror*, Random House, 2002.

111 Jane Mayer, 'The Predator War,' *The New Yorker*, October 26, 2009.

112 Jo Becker and Scott Shane, 'Secret "Kill List" Proves a Test of Obama's Principles and Will,' *The New York Times*, May 29, 2012.

113 Marc Ambinder, 'The Secret Team That Killed bin Laden,' *National Journal*, May 3, 2011.

114 Gretchen Gavett, 'What is the Secretive U.S. "Kill/Capture" Campaign?,' PBS: Public Broadcasting Service.

115 Ibid.

116 James Risen and Mark Mazzetti, 'C.I.A. Said to Use Outsiders to Put Bombs on Drones,' *The New York Times*, August 20, 2009.

117 Karen DeYoung, 'US Increases Yemen Drone Strikes,' *The Washington Post*, September 17, 2011.

118 'Air Raid Kills Yemeni Mediator,' Al Jazeera English, May 25, 2010.

119 Bill Roggio, 'Yemeni Airstrike Kills Deputy Governor, Al Qaeda Operative,' *The Long War Journal*, May 25, 2010.

120 CBS/AP, 'Al Qaeda's Anwar al-Awlaki Killed in Yemen,' CBS News, September 30, 2011.

121 Peter Finn and Greg Miller, 'Anwar al-Awlaki's Family Speaks Out Against His Son's Death in Airstrike,' *The Washington Post*, October 17, 2011.

122 'Wikileaks Cable Corroborates Evidence of US Airstrikes in Yemen,' Amnesty International, December 1, 2010.

123 Spencer Ackerman, 'CIA's Drone Join Shadow War Over Yemen,' Wired.com, June 14, 2011.

124 Jim Lobe, 'US: Expanding Network of Drone Bases To Hit Somalia, Yemen,' IPS Inter Press Service, September 21, 2011.

125 Department of Defense, 'News Transcript: Deputy Secretary Wolfowitz Interview with Sam Tannenhaus, Vanity Fair,' The Official Home of the Department of Defense, May 9, 2003.

126 Nick Turse, 'The Forty-Year Drone War,' TomDispatch, January 24, 2010.

127 'Al Dhafra Air Base,' GlobalSecurity.org, May 7, 2011.

128 Greg Miller and Craig Whitlock, 'U.S. Building Secret Drone Bases in Africa, Arabian Peninsula, Officials Say,' *The Washington Post*, September 20, 2011.

129 Craig Whitlock, 'Remote U.S. Base at Core of Secret Operations,' *The Washington Post*, October 25, 2012.

130 'Press Briefing by Press Secretary Jay Carney,' The White House, October 28, 2011.

131 Jim Lobe, 'US: Expanding Network of Drone Bases To Hit Somalia, Yemen,' IPS Inter Press Service, September 21, 2011.

132 'Seychelles: Ocean Look Tops Agenda During Presidential Meeting,' *The Washington Post*, n.d.

133 'U.S. Building Secret Drone Bases in Africa, Arabian Peninsula, Officials Say,' *The Washington Post*, September 20, 2011.

134 'Uganda and Burundi to Get US Drones to Fight Islamists,' BBC News, June 28, 2011.

135 Spencer Ackerman, 'Libya: The Real U.S. Drone War,' Wired.com, October 20, 2011.

136 Greg Jaffe, 'Fleet of U.S. Drones Now Based in Turkey,' *The Washington Post*, November 14, 2011.

137 *Unmanned Daily News*, August 16, 2011.

138 'The Future of War: Keynote Address at the CSIS Global Security Forum 2011,' United States Department of Defense, June 8, 2011.

139 'Agencies Could Improve Information Sharing and End-Use Monitoring on Unmanned Aerial Vehicle Exports,' Government Accountability Office, July 2012.

140 Ibid.

141 Anshel Pfeffer, 'WikiLeaks: IDF Uses Drones to Assassinate Gaza Militants,' *Haaretz Israeli News*, February 9, 2011.

142 Scott Wilson, 'In Gaza, Lives Shaped by Drones,' *The Washington Post*, December 3, 2011.

143 Chris Cole, 'Drone Wars Briefing,' January 2012 p. 6.

144 Robert Wall, 'Watchkeeper Misses Key Schedule Milestone,' *Aviation Week*, January 11, 2012.

145 Nick Hopkins, 'Afghan Civilians Killed by RAF Drone,' *The Guardian*, July 5, 2011.

146 Ibid.

147 'Iraq Insurgents Hack into Video Feeds from US Drones,' BBC News, December 17, 2009.

148 'Syrian Downing of Israeli Drone Raises Specter of Syrian Scuds,' *DEBKAfile* Exclusive, 2006.

149 'Iranian Drone "Shot Down in Iraq,"' BBC News, March 16, 2009.

150 'Agencies Could Improve Information Sharing and End-Use Monitoring on Unmanned Aerial Vehicle Exports,' Government Accountability Office, July 2012.

151 Mark T. Maybury, 'Remotely Piloted Aircraft,' US Air Force, September 27, 2011.

152 William Booth, 'More Predator Drones Fly U.S.-Mexico Border,' *The Washington Post*, December 21, 2011.

153 Charlie Savage, 'U.S. Drug Enforcement Agency Expands War on Drugs,' *The New York Times*, November 6, 2011.

154 'Membership' Congressional Unmanned Systems Caucus Committee.

155 Alan Levin, 'Commercial Drones: A Dogfight at the FAA,' *Business Week*, February 9, 2012.

156 Brian Bennett, 'Police Employ Predator Drone Spy Planes on Home Front,' *The Los Angeles Times*, December 10, 2011.

157 'Drone May be Coming to Miami-Dade,' WSVN 7NEWS Miami/Ft. Lauderdale, January 6, 2011.

158 Tim Elfrink, 'MDPD is First Force to Get FAA Clearance to Fly Drones at Crime Scenes,' The Miami New Times' Blogs, November 15, 2011.

159 'Miami Police Could Become First to Use Drones in a U.S. City,' TPMMuckraker, January 7, 2011.

160 Stephen Dean, 'New Police Drone Near Houston Could Carry Weapons,' Click 2 Houston | KPRC Local 2, November 10, 2011.

161 'Talk of Drones Patrolling U.S. Skies Spawns Anxiety,' *USA Today*, June 19, 2012.

162 Richard M. Thompson, 'Drones in Domestic Surveillance Operations: Fourth Amendment Implications and Legislative Responses,' *Congressional Research Service*, September 6, 2012.

163 Jay Stanley and Catherine Crump, 'Protecting Privacy From Aerial Surveillance,' ACLU, December 2011, p 1.

164 Jay Stanley and Catherine Crump, 'Protecting Privacy From Aerial Surveillance,' ACLU, December 2011, p 11.

165 Glenn Greenwald, 'NPR's Domestic Drone Commercial,' Salon.com, December 6, 2011.

166 'As The Drone Flies...,' The Nader Page, Nader.org, September 26, 2011.

167 CBS/AP, 'Mass. Musician Accused of D.C. Terrorist Plot,' CBS News, September 28, 2011.

168 Business Wire, 'AeroVironment, Inc.: U.S. Army Awards AeroVironment $4.9 Million Contract for Switchblade Agile Munition Systems and Services,' AeroVironment, Inc., September 1, 2011.

169 David Zucchino, 'Drone Pilot Fights Afghan War from Nevada Base,' *AZ Central*, February 24, 2010.

170 Nick Turse, 'America's Secret Empire of Drone Bases,' *The Huffington Post*, October 17, 2011.

171 Thom Shanker and Matt Richtel, 'Military Struggles to Harness a Flood of Data,' *The New York Times*, January 17, 2011.

172 Ibid.

173 Gareth Porter, 'CIA's Push for Drone War Driven by Internal Needs,' IPS Inter Press Service, September 5, 2011.

174 United Nations General Assembly: Human Rights Council, 'Report of the Special Rapporteur on Extrajudicial, Summary or Arbitrary Executions, Philip Alston,' Fourteenth Session, May 23, 2010.

175 Christian Caryl, 'Predators and Robots at War,' *The New York Review of Books*, September 29, 2011.

176 P.W. Singer, *Wired for War: The Robotics Revolution and Conflict in the Twenty-First Century*. New York: Penguin Press, 2009, Ch. 3, p. 68.

177 P. W. Singer, *Wired for War*. New York, 2009, p. 332.

178 Greg Jaffe, 'Combat Generation: Drone Operators Climb on Winds of Change in the Air Force,' *The Washington Post*, February 27, 2010.

179 Ibid.

180 Elisabeth Bumiller, 'Air Force Drone Operators Show High Levels of Stress,' *The New York Times*, December 19, 2011.

181 'Report on Operating Next-Generation Remotely Piloted Aircraft in Irregular Warfare,' United States Airforce Scientific Advisory Board, April 2011.

182 Elisabeth Bumiller, 'Air Force Drone Operators Show High Levels of Stress,' *The New York Times*, December 19, 2011.

183 Associated Press, 'Air Force Makes Push For Drone Operators,' CBS News, October 23, 2008.

184 David S. Cloud, 'Contractors' Role Grows in Drone Missions, Worrying Some in the Military,' McClatchy D.C., December 29, 2011.

185 Mark Thompson, 'Flying Air Force Drones: Pilots No Longer Required,' TIME.com, September 18, 2008.

186 Associated Press, 'Remote-control Warriors Suffer War Stress,' MSNBC, August 7, 2008.

187 Al Jazeera English, 'America's Use for Domestic Drones,' YouTube, December 7, 2011.

188 Matt J. Martin and Charles W. Sasser, *Predator: The Remote-control Air War Over Iraq and Afghanistan: A Pilot's Story*. Minneapolis, MN: Zenith Press, 2010 Ch. 20, p. 211.

189 'Interview with a Drone Pilot: "It Is Not a Video Game,"' Spiegel Online, Nachrichten, March 12, 2010.

190 David S. Cloud, 'Afghanistan Predator Drones: Despite High-Tech Tools, a Fatal Error,' *The Los Angeles Times*, April 10, 2011.

191 'Drone Pilot Kills Afghani Militants from Nevada Control Centre,' YouTube, October 23, 2009.

192 Elisabeth Bumiller, 'A Day Job Waiting for a Kill Shot a World Away,' *The New York Times*, July 29, 2012.

193 Tom Bowman, 'Predator Pilots Engage in Remote Control Combat,' NPR, September 4, 2007.

194 Rachel Martin, 'Report: High Levels Of "Burnout" In U.S. Drone Pilots,' NPR, December 19, 2011.

195 Elisabeth Bumiller, 'A Day Job Waiting for a Kill Shot a World Away,' *The New York Times*, July 29, 2012.

196 Elisabeth Bumiller, 'Air Force Drone Operators Show High Levels of Stress,' *The New York Times*, December 19, 2011.

197 Sally B. Donnelly, 'Long-Distance Warriors,' TIME.com, December 4, 2005.

198 Megan McCloskey, 'Two Worlds of a Drone Pilot,' Military.com, October 27, 2009.

199 'Interview with a Drone Pilot: "It Is Not a Video Game,"' Spiegel Online, Nachrichten, March 12, 2010.

200 Sally B. Donnelly, 'Long-Distance Warriors,' TIME.com, December 4, 2005.

201 Jefferson Morley, 'Boredom, Terror, Deadly Mistakes: Secrets of the New Drone War,' *Salon*, April 3, 2012.
202 Matt J. Martin and Charles W. Sasser, *Predator: The Remote-control Air War Over Iraq and Afghanistan: A Pilot's Story*. Minneapolis, MN: Zenith Press, 2010 Ch. 10, p. 112.
203 Thom Shanker and Matt Richtel, 'Military Struggles to Harness a Flood of Data,' *The New York Times*, January 17, 2011.
204 Joe Pappalardo, 'The Future For UAVs in the U.S. Air Force,' *Popular Mechanics*, February 26, 2010.
205 P.W. Singer, *Wired for War: Robotics Revolution and Conflict in the Twenty-first Century*. New York: Penguin, 2009, accessed via Google Books.
206 Peter Finn, 'U.S. Moves Towards Robotic Warfare,' *The Fiscal Times*, September 20, 2011.
207 Alex Rodriguez and David Zucchino, 'U.S. Drone Attacks in Pakistan Get Mixed Response,' *The Los Angeles Times*, May 2, 2010.
208 'The Bush Years: Pakistan Strikes 2004–2009,' The Bureau of Investigative Journalism, August 10, 2011.
209 'Drones Are Successful Tool in War on Terror,' *The Wall Street Journal*, January 9, 2010.
210 Chris Woods, 'Number of CIA Drone Strikes in Pakistan Hits 300,' TBIJ, October 14, 2011.
211 Scott Shane, 'C.I.A. Claim of No Civilian Deaths From Drones Is Disputed,' *The New York Times*, August 11, 2011.
212 'The Year of the Drone,' Counterterrorism Strategy Initiative, NewAmerica.net.
213 Chris Woods, 'Number of CIA Drone Strikes in Pakistan Hits 300,' TBIJ, October 14, 2011.
214 Saeed Shah and Peter Beaumont, 'US Drone Strikes in Pakistan Claiming Many Civilian Victims, says Campaigner,' *The Guardian*, July 17, 2011.
215 Pir Zubair Shah, Sabrina Tavernise and Mark Mazzetti, 'Taliban Leader in Pakistan Is Reportedly Killed,' *The New York Times*, August 8, 2009.
216 Jane Mayer, 'The Risks of the C.I.A.'s Predator Drones,' *The New Yorker*, October 26, 2009.
217 Carlotta Gall, 'Pakistani Militant Chief Is Reported Dead,' *The New York Times*, June 4, 2011.
218 Salman Masood and David E. Sanger, 'Standoff on Pakistan Naval Base Ends,' *The New York Times*, May 24, 2011.
219 Story provided by lawyer Shahzad Akbar, January 29, 2012.
220 Legal Notice served on behalf of Karim Khan to US Consulate in Islamabad by Mirza and Associates, provided by Karim Khan's legal counsel.
221 Declan Walsh, 'Pakistani Journalist Sues CIA for Drone Strike That Killed Relatives,' *The Guardian*, December 13, 2010.
222 Ibid.

223 Ansar Abbasi, 'Local CIA Chief May Face Case Against Drone Attacks,' *News International*, December 1, 2010.
224 Pratap Chatterjee, 'Bureau Reporter Meets 16-year-old Three Days Before US Drone Kills Him,' TBIJ, November 4, 2011.
225 Ibid.
226 Clive Stafford Smith, 'In Pakistan, Drones Kill Our Innocent Allies,' *The New York Times*, November 4, 2011.
227 Nick Schifrin, 'Tariq Khan Killed by CIA Drone,' ABC News, December 30, 2011.
228 Interview with Pratap Chatterjee, January 16, 2012.
229 Adam Entous, Siobhan Gorman and Julian E. Barnes, 'U.S. Tightens Drone Rules for Its Pakistan Attacks,' *The Wall Street Journal*, November 4, 2011.
230 'Living Under Drones: Death, Injury and Trauma to Civilians From US Drone Practices in Pakistan,' Stanford University Law School and New York University School of Law, September 25, 2012.
231 Ibid.
232 Ibid.
233 Alex Rodriguez, 'Pakistan Death Squads Go After Informants to U.S. Drone Program,' *The Los Angeles Times*, December 28, 2011.
234 Ibid.
235 Jane Perlez, 'Karachi Turns Deadly Amid Pakistan's Rivalries,' *The New York Times*, November 19, 2010.
236 Greg Miller, 'Al-Qaeda Targets Dwindle as Group Shrinks,' *The Washington Post*, November 22, 2011.
237 Shatha Al-Harazi, 'Yemenis Question the Killing of 16-year-old Al-Awlaki's Son,' *Yemen Times*, October 19, 2011.
238 'Drones shape life in Gaza,' *The Washington Post*, December 3, 2011.
239 'Precisely Wrong: Gaza Civilians Killed by Israeli Drone-Launched Missiles,' Human Rights Watch, June 2009.
240 Yotam Feldman and Uri Blau, 'Consent and Advise,' *Haaretz*, January 29, 2009.
241 Tara McKelvey, 'Inside the Killing Machine,' *The Daily Beast*, February 13, 2011.
242 Jane Mayer, 'The Predator War,' *The New Yorker*, February 26, 2009.
243 Harold Hongju Koh, 'The Obama administration and International Law,' U.S. Department of State, March 25, 2010.
244 Hunter Miller, 'British-American Diplomacy: The Caroline Case,' Avalon Project - Yale Law School.
245 Oliver Burkeman and Julian Borger, 'War Critics Astonished as US Hawk Admits Invasion was Illegal,' *The Guardian*, November 20, 2003.
246 Declan Walsh, 'US Extends Drone Strikes to Somalia,' *The Guardian*, June 30, 2011.
247 Greg Miller, 'Under Obama, an Emerging Global Apparatus for Drone Killing,' *The Washington Post*, December 27, 2011.

248 'The Laws of War,' Human Rights Investigations, Last updated: April 30, 2011.
249 Chris Woods and Christina Lamb, 'Obama Terror Drones: CIA Tactics in Pakistan Include Targeting Rescuers and Funerals,' Bureau of Investigative Journalism, February 4, 2012.
250 'Living Under Drones,' Stanford University Law School and New York University School of Law, September 25, 2012.
251 Jack Serle, 'UN Expert Labels CIA Tactic Exposed by Bureau "a War Crime,"' Bureau of Investigative Journalism, June 21, 2012.
252 'Court Dismisses Targeted Killing Case On Procedural Grounds Without Addressing Merits,' ACLU Press Release, December 7, 2010.
253 Daphne Eviatar, 'Pressure Mounts on Obama Administration to Release Legal Justification for al-Awlaki Killing,' *The Huffington Post*, October 6, 2011.
254 Noah Feldman, 'Obama Team's Al-Awlaki Memo Furthered Bush Legacy,' Bloomberg, October 17, 2011.
255 Megan Mitchell, 'Osama bin Laden Won't Be Brought in Alive,' U.S. Congressman John Culberson: 7th District of Texas, March 16, 2010.
256 Josh Gerstein, 'Osama bin Laden Won't be Brought in Alive,' Politico.com, March 16, 2010.
257 Yochi J. Dreazen, Aamer Madhani and Marc Ambinder, 'For Obama, Killing – Not Capturing – bin Laden Was Goal,' NationalJournal.com, May 4, 2011.
258 Human Rights Council, 'Report of the Special Rapporteur on Extrajudicial, Summary or Arbitrary Executions, Philip Alston,' United Nations General Assembly – Fourteenth Session, May 23, 2010.
259 Mary Ellen O'Connell, 'Lawful Use of Combat Drones – Hearing: Rise of the Drones II: Examining the Legality of Unmanned Targeting,' Subcommittee on National Security and Foreign Affairs, Congress of the United States: House of Representatives, April 28, 2010.
260 'ACLU Letter to President Obama,' American Civil Liberties Union, April 28, 2010.
261 Scott Shane, 'Leaked Cables Offer Raw Look at U.S. Diplomacy,' *The New York Times*, December 28, 2011.
262 Delcan Walsh, 'WikiLeaks Cables: US and Pakistan Play Down Impact of "Mischief,"' *The Guardian*, December 1, 2010.
263 'Pakistan Says U.S. Drones in its Air Space Will be Shot Down,' MSNBC, December 10, 2011.
264 Chris Woods, 'CIA Drone Strikes Violate Pakistan's Sovereignty, Says Senior Diplomat,' *The Guardian*, August 2, 2012.
265 Gary Solis, 'CIA Drone Attacks Produce America's Own Unlawful Combatants,' *The Washington Post*, March 11, 2010.
266 James Risen and Mark Mazzetti, 'NY Times Advertisement,' NY Times Advertisement, August 21, 2009.

267 David S. Cloud, 'Contractors' Role Grows in Drone Missions, Worrying Some in the Military,' *The New York Times*, December 29, 2011.
268 Ibid.
269 'UN Human Rights Expert Challenges "Targeted Killing" Policies,' Office of the High Commissioner for Human Rights, October 20, 2011.
270 'Q & A: US Targeted Killings and International Law,' Human Rights Watch, December 19, 2011.
271 Charles Davis, 'U.S./CUBA: Justice Not So Blind in Politically Charged Cases,' IPS Inter Press Service, January 29, 2008.
272 'Collateral Damage,' Wikipedia.
273 David Rohde, 'The Drone War,' *Reuters Magazine*, January 17, 2012.
274 P.W. Singer, 'Wired for War,' *Wilson Quarterly*, Winter 2009.
275 Teri Schultz, 'Meet the Pilots Who Fly America's Drones,' *GlobalPost*, December 16, 2011.
276 'No-fly Zone,' Wikipedia.
277 Barack Obama, 'Letter from the President on the War Powers Resolution,' The White House, June 15, 2011.
278 'United States Activities in Libya,' Foreign Policy Files, June 15, 2011.
279 C. J. Chivers and Eric Schmitt, 'Scores of Unintended Casualties in NATO War in Libya,' *The New York Times*, December 18, 2011.
280 Joshua Foust, 'Unaccountable Killing Machines: The True Cost of U.S. Drones,' *The Atlantic*, December 30, 2011.
281 United Kingdom Ministry of Defence, 'The UK Approach to Unmanned Aircraft Systems,' Joint Doctrine Note 2/11, Section 5–9.
282 Jane Mayer, 'The Predator War,' *The New Yorker*, October 26, 2009.
283 Deputy Foreign Minister Ahmed Yusef, interview by author, Gaza, June 2, 2009.
284 'Remote-Control Warfare,' *The Christian Century*, May 2005.
285 Glenn Greenwald, 'Joe Klein's Sociopathic Defense of Drone Killings of Children,' *The Guardian*, October 23, 2012.
286 Paul F.M. Zahl, Daniel M. Bell Jr. and Brian Stiltner, 'Drones: Is It Wrong to Kill by Remote Control?' ChristianityToday.com, August 2011.
287 Ben Austen, 'The Terminator Scenario: Are We Giving Our Military Machines Too Much Power?' *Popular Science*, December 2010.
288 Peter Finn, 'A Future for Drones: Automated Killing,' *The Washington Post*, September 15, 2011.
289 Noel Sharkey, 'Automated warfare: Lessons Learned From the Drones,' *Journal of Law, Information and Science*, August 11, 2011.
290 Lt. Col. Dave Grossman, 'Hope on the Battlefield,' Greater Good, Summer 2007.
291 Rev. John Dear, 'A Peace Movement Victory in Court,' Common Dreams, September 18, 2010.
292 Ibid.
293 Kathy Kelly, 'The Predators: Where is Your Democracy?' Voices for Creative Nonviolence, May 9, 2011.

294 Rachel Stern, 'Ithaca Group Walking to Syracuse to Protest US Drone Missiles,' Voices for Creative Nonviolence, April 2011.
295 Andy Beckett, 'Protest and Survive: The Greenham Veteran who Refuses to go Away,' *The Guardian*, November 17, 2011.
296 'Piñon Canyon Expansion Parcel Map,' Grassland Trust and Not 1 More Acre.
297 Chris Hellman, 'Press Room,' National Priorities Project, February 14, 2011.
298 'Integrated Solutions News,' *The Sacramento Bee.*
299 'James Hill News,' *The Sacramento Bee.*
300 CCR and the ACLU v. OFAC & Al-Aulaqi v. Obama, Center for Constitutional Rights.
301 Michael Ratner, 'The Extrajudicial Drone Murder of US Citizen Anwar al-Awlaki,' AlterNet, October 2, 2011.
302 'Who Is Flying Unmanned Aircraft in the U.S.?,' Electronic Frontier Foundation, January 10, 2010.
303 'Q & A: US Targeted Killings and International Law,' Human Rights Watch, December 19, 2011.
304 Mary Ellen O'Connell, 'Lawful Use of Combat Drones,' Hearing: Rise of the Drones II: Examining the Legality of Unmanned Targeting from Subcommittee on National Security and Foreign Affairs, Washington, D.C., April 28, 2010.
305 'Defense Department Does Not Compile Total Number Of Civilians Killed In Drone Attacks,' American Civil Liberties Union, March 22, 2011.
306 Chris Rogers, 'Report: Pakistan 2010,' CIVIC: Campaign for Innocent Victims in Conflict, October 2010.
307 Maria Keenan, 'Pakistan: Compensation Promised to Civilian Drone Victims,' CIVIC: Campaign for Innocent Victims in Conflict, March 28, 2011.
308 David Hookes, 'Armed Drones: How Remote-Controlled, High-Tech Weapons are Used Against the Poor,' Scientists for Global Responsibility, Winter 2011.
309 Chris Cole, 'Convenient Killing: Armed Drones and the "Playstation" Mentality,' The Fellowship of Reconciliation, England, 2010.
310 'Current campaign: Drone Wars,' Fellowship of Reconciliation, England.
311 Paul McGowan, Interview by Alli McCracken, Online, December 7, 2011.
312 Jim Wright, Interview by Alli McCracken, Online, December 5, 2011.
313 'ICRAC,' ICRAC - International Committee for Robot Arms Control.
314 'ICBL - International Campaign to Ban Landmines,' ICBL.
315 Ibid.
316 Ibid.
317 Ibid.
318 Jeff Hawkins, Personal Interview by Author, Washington, D.C., November 15, 2011.
319 Peter Asaro, personal website.

320 'Losing Humanity: The Case Against Killer Robots,' Human Rights Watch, November 19, 2012.
321 Nick Mottern, Personal interview by author, Washington, D.C., January 4, 2012.
322 Tara McKelvey, 'Inside the Killing Machine,' *Newsweek*, February 13, 2011.
323 Ibid.
324 Noah Shachtman, 'CIA Chief: Drones "Only Game in Town" for Stopping Al Qaeda,' *Wired*, May 19, 2009.
325 David Kilcullen and Andrew McDonald Exum, 'Op-Ed Contributors: Death From Above, Outrage Down Below,' *The New York Times*, May 17, 2009.
326 David Rohde, 'Held by the Taliban: A Times Reporter's Account. A Five-Part Series,' *The New York Times*, October 18, 2009.
327 'Pakistani Public Opinion Ever More Critical of U.S.,' Pew Research, June 27, 2012.
328 Karen DeYoung and Karin Brulliard, 'U.S. Breach with Pakistan Shows Imbalance Between Diplomatic Security Goals,' *The Washington Post*, December 4, 2011.
329 William Astore, 'Fighting 1 Percent Wars,' *TomDispatch*, December 8, 2011.
330 Jo Becker and Scott Shane, 'Secret "Kill List" Proves a Test of Obama's Principles and Will,' *The New York Times*, May 29, 2012.
331 Seth Jones and Martin Libicki, *How Terrorist Groups End: Lessons for Countering Al Qaida*. Rand Publishing, 2008.
332 Jimmy Carter, 'A Cruel and Unusual Record,' *The New York Times*, June 24, 2012.
333 *The New York Times*, June 6, 2011.
334 Andrew Stobo Sniderman and Mark Harris, 'Drones for Human Rights,' *The New York Times*, January 30, 2012.